Joseph Masters

A Catalogue of Books and Tracts, Churc Music and Other Musical Works

Joseph Masters

A Catalogue of Books and Tracts, Churc Music and Other Musical Works

ISBN/EAN: 9783742817143

Manufactured in Europe, USA, Canada, Australia, Japa

Cover: Foto ©Angelika Wolter / pixelio.de

Manufactured and distributed by brebook publishing software
(www.brebook.com)

Joseph Masters

A Catalogue of Books and Tracts, Churc Music and Other Musical Works

A CATALOGUE

OF

BOOKS AND TRACTS,

CHURCH MUSIC,

AND OTHER

𝕸usical 𝕮orks Sacred and Secular,

WITH A

CLASSIFIED PRICE LIST OF BOOKS

SUITABLE FOR

SCHOOL REWARDS AND LENDING LIBRARIES,

PUBLISHED BY

JOSEPH MASTERS & CO.,

78, NEW BOND STREET,

LONDON.

PRINTING.

J. MASTERS & Co. beg to state that their PRINTING OFFICE is extensive, and well supplied with all that is necessary for the execution of every description of Printing; and that they give to all works entrusted to their care the best possible attention, so as to ensure the greatest accuracy in their production. Nearly the whole of the books comprised in the accompanying Catalogue, including almost every variety of style and type, have been produced in their own Printing Office. To these they refer as offering a sufficient guarantee of their facilities for undertaking any kind of work.

CLASSIFIED INDEX.

REWARD BOOKS.

SCRIPTURE READINGS.

SERMONS.

TALES AND ALLEGORIES.

THEOLOGICAL

WORKS PUBLISHED BY J. MASTERS & CO.

ACTS OF THE APOSTLES, The. An Exposition of the leading Events recorded in that Book. Cloth, 1s.

ADAMS, The Rev. W.
Sylvio. An Allegory. Chiefly from the MS. of the late Rev. William Adams, Author of the "Shadow of the Cross," "Old Man's Home," &c. Edited by C. Warren Adams. 8s.

The Fall of Crœsus: a Story from Herodotus. 2s. 6d.

ADAMS.—Cunningham; or, the Missionary. By C. P. Adams. 1s.

ALEXANDER, Mrs. C. F.
Hymns for Little Children. 16mo., wrapper, 6d.; cloth, 1s.; French morocco, 2s.
—— Royal 32mo., wrapper, 3d.; cloth, 6d.
—— Set to Music by Dr. Gauntlett. Fcap. 4to., wrapper, 3s. 6d.; cloth, gilt edges, 4s.
—— Set to Music by E. C. A. Chepmell. Parts I. and II. 1s. each.
—— Fcap. 4to. Illustrated with Forty-one full page engravings, by Messrs. Dalziel. Printed on toned paper, and handsomely bound in cloth extra, gilt edges. 3s. 6d.

Hymns, Descriptive and Devotional, for the use of Schools. Royal 32mo., 2d.

Moral Songs, with Thirty-nine Vignette Illustrations. 18mo., wrapper, 2d.; cloth, 1s.; French morocco, 2s.
—— royal 32mo., wrapper, 3d.

Narrative Hymns for Village Schools. 16mo., wrapper, 2d.
—— Set to Music for one or two voices, by A. F. Fcap. 4to., wrapper, 2s. 6d.

Poems on Subjects in the Old Testament. Parts I. and II., each 6d., wrapper; in one vol., cloth, 1s. 6d.

The Baron's Little Daughter, and other Tales in Prose and Verse. Fourth edition. 18mo., cloth, 2s. 6d.

The Lord of the Forest and his Vassals. An Allegory. Fourth edition. 16mo., cloth, 2s. 6d.

ALICE BERESFORD; a Tale of Home Life. By the Author of "Tales of Kirkbeck," &c. 2nd edit. Fcap. 8vo. cloth, 3s. 6d.

AMY, THE KING'S DAUGHTER. A Tale. 1s., paper 6d.

ANDREWES (Bp.)—A Manual of Private Devotions, containing Prayers for each Day in the Week, Devotions for the Holy Communion, and for the Sick. 6d.; pd. cloth.

ANTHEMS, Words of, as used in Churches. 1s.

APPLE BLOSSOM, The; or, a Mother's Legacy. A Tale. By Cousin Titian. 3s. 6d.

ARCHIE'S AMBITION. 18mo. cloth, 1s.

ARDEN.—Manual of Catechetical Instruction, arranged by the Rev. G. Arden. 2s.

A Supplemental Catechism on the Holy Catholic Church. 1d., or 9d. per doz.

ASHLEY, The Rev. J. M.
The Victory of the Spirit: a Course of Short Sermons by way of Commentary on the Eighth Chapter of S. Paul's Epistle to the Romans. Fcap. 8vo., cloth, 2s.

Thirteen Sermons from the Quaresimale of Quirico Rossi. Translated from the Italian. Edited by J. M. Ashley, B.C.L. Fcap. 8vo., cloth, 3s. 6d.

ATHANASIUS, and other Poems. By a Fellow of a College. Fcap. 8vo., 2s.

ATKINS.—Three Essays on the Eternal Sonship of Christ; The Kingdom of Heaven; and the Resurrection. By the late Rev. W. H. Atkins, A.M. 3s. 6d.

B

BAGOT.—Selections from the Letters of S. Francis de Sales. Translated from the French by Mrs. C. W. Bagot. Revised by a Priest of the English Church. 4th edit. Fcap. 8vo., cloth, 1s. 6d.

BADGER.—The Nestorians and their Rituals. By the Rev. G. P. Badger, M.A. 2 vols., with numerous Illustrations and maps. 21s.

BAINES, The Rev. J.
Tales of the Empire, or Scenes from the History of the House of Hapsburg. 1s. 6d., paper 1s.
The Life of William Laud, Archbishop and Martyr. Fcap. 8vo., 2s. 6d.
Conversations on the History of England, for the use of Children. By C. A. B. Edited by the Rev. J. Baines. 18mo., 2s. 6d.

BAPTISMAL VOWS; or, the Feast of S. Barnabas. A Tale. 18mo., 1s.

BARING-GOULD, The Rev. S.
One Hundred Sketches of Sermons for Extempore Preachers. 2nd edition. Crown 8vo., 6s.
Village Conferences on the Creed. Crown 8vo., 2s. 6d.

BAYLISS.—Loving Service; or, a Sister's Influence. By Eliza A. Bayliss. Fcap. 8vo., 2s. 6d.

BEGINNINGS OF EVIL, The: being Tales on the Ten Commandments. By M. M. S. 18mo., 2s. 6d.

BELLARMINE.—The Seven Words from the Cross. A Devotional Commentary. By Bellarmine. 1s.

BENN, Mary.
The Solitary; or, a Lay from the West. With other Poems in English and Latin. 2s. 6d.
Lays of the Hebrews, and other Poems. 2s.

BENNETT.—Tales of a London Parish, &c., by the author of "Tales of Kirkbeck." Edited by the Rev. W. J. E. Bennett. 18mo. 2s. 6d.

S. BERNARD.—The Sweet Rhythm of S. Bernard on the Most Holy Name of Jesus. Newly done into English. 2d.

BEST.—A Plea for Daily Public Worship; being extracts from "An Essay on the Daily Service of the Church of England. By William Best, D.D." Published in 1746. 2d.

BEZANT.—Geographical Questions, classed under heads and interspersed with History and General Information. By J. Bezant. 1s. KEY to ditto, 2s.

BINGHAM.—Sermons on Easter Subjects. By the Rev. W. P. S. Bingham, M.A. Fcap. 8vo. cloth, 4s. 6d.

BIRTHDAY, The. By the author of "Clifton," &c. 1s. 6d.

BISHOP'S LITTLE DAUGHTER, The. Fifth edition. 18mo., 1s.

BLACK, The Rev. C. I.
A Little Primer of Christian Worship and Doctrine. Cloth, 2d.
Messias and Anti-Messias. A Prophetical Exposition, to which are added Two Homilies on the Body of Christ. 8vo. 5s.
A Short Manual, Expository and Devotional, on the Prayer of the New Covenant. Fcap. 8vo., 2s. 6d.

BLACKMORE, The Rev. R. W.
The Doctrine of the Russian Church, &c. Translated from the Slavonic-Russian by the Rev. R. W. Blackmore. 8vo. 8s.
Harmony of Anglican Doctrines with those of the Catholic and Apostolic Church of the East. 8vo. 3s.
History of the Church of Russia, by A. N. Mouravieff. Translated by the Rev. R. W. Blackmore, M.A. 8vo. 10s. 6d.

BLUNT.—The Atonement and the Atonement-maker. By the Rev. J. H. Blunt. Fcap. 8vo., 2s. 6d.

BONUS, A.
Beatrice; a Tale of the Early Christians. 1s. 6d.
River Reeds. Poems. Fcap. 8vo., 2s. 6d.

BOOK OF GENESIS, The. An Exposition of the Leading Events recorded in it. Fcap. 8vo., cloth, 1s.

BOOK OF COMMON PRAYER, The, of 1662, according to the Sealed Copy in the Tower. Printed in red and black, with the old Elzevir type, antique cloth, 10s. 6d.; calf, 14s.; morocco, 17s. 6d.; antique calf, 16s. and 21s., antique morocco, 21s., &c.

BOOK OF COMMON PRAYER, The, according to the use of the Church of Scotland, Roan gilt, 3s. 6d.

BOOK OF CHURCH HISTORY, founded on the Rev. W. Palmer's "Ecclesiastical History." 18mo., 1s. Fifth Edition.

BOOK OF FAMILY PRAYERS, collected from the Public Liturgy of the Church of England. By the Rector of Durham. 2s.

BOOK OF STRANGE PREACHERS as ordered by the 33rd Canon, etc., cs. 6d.

BOWDLER, The Rev. T.
A Few Words of Family Instruction, introductory to "Prayers for a Christian Household." Fcap. 8vo., cloth, 1s. 6d.
Sermons on the Privileges, Responsibilities, and Duties of Members of the Gospel Covenant. 2 vols., post 8vo., cloth, 7s. 6d. each.
Prayers for a Christian Household, chiefly taken from the Scriptures, from the Ancient Liturgies, and the Book of Common Prayer. Fcap. 8vo., cloth, 3s. 6d.

BOWDLER, Mrs. H. M.—Sermons on the Doctrines and Duties of Christianity. 6th edit. To which is prefixed an Essay on the Proper Employment of Time, Talents, Fortune, &c. Fcp. 8vo., 5s.

BRECHIN, The Bishop of.
A Primary Charge delivered to the Clergy of his Diocese, at the Annual Synod of 1857. Third edition, 1s.
The Christian's Converse. A practical treatise, adapted by the Bishop of Brechin. 6d. cloth. 6d. roan.
Meditations on the Passion of our Lord Jesus Christ, according to the Four Evangelists, by the Abbot of Monte Cassino. Edited by the Bishop of Brechin. 18mo., 3s.
Meditations on the Suffering Life of our Lord. Translated from Pinart, by the late Lady Eleanor Law. Edited by the Bishop of Brechin. 4th edit. 4s.; calf antique, 10s.
Memoriale Vitæ Sacerdotalis; or, Solemn Warnings of the Great Shepherd, Jesus Christ, to the Clergy of His Holy Church. Translated from the Latin by the Bishop of Brechin. Second edition. Fcap. 8vo., 3s. 6d.
Nourishment of the Christian Soul. Translated from Pinart, by the late Lady Eleanor Law. Edited by the Bishop of Brechin. 4th edit. 4s.; calf antique, 10s.
The Mirror of Young Christians. Translated from the French, by the late Lady Eleanor Law. Edited by the Bishop of Brechin. With Engravings. 3s. 6d. Morocco antique, 7s. Cheap edition, 1s. The Engravings separately, 6d.
Theological Defence for the Bishop of Brechin on a Presentment by the Rev. W. Henderson and others, on certain points concerning the doctrine of the Holy Eucharist. 8vo., 5s.
The Scottish Communion Office in Greek. 18mo., 2s.
Are you being Converted? Sermons on Serious Subjects. Third Edit. Fcap. 8vo., 3s.
The Waning of Opportunities, and other Sermons. Practical and Doctrinal. Fcap. 8vo., 3s. 6d.
Sermons on the Grace of God, and other Cognate Subjects. 3s. 6d.
A Commentary on the Litany. Fcap. 8vo., cl., 3s. 6d.
A Commentary on the Te Deum, from ancient sources. 3s., cloth; cheap edition, 1s.
A Commentary on the Canticles used in the Prayer Book. 2s., cheap edition, 1s.
Commentary on the Seven Penitential Psalms, from ancient sources. Cloth, 2d. and 1s.
The Seal of the Lord: A Catechism on Confirmation, with appropriate Devotions. 1½d., or 10s. 6d. per 100.
Catechism to be learnt before the Church Catechism. 1s. per 100.
The Holiness of the Human Body, and the Duties of Society. 2d. each.
A Memoir of the Pious Life and Holy Death of Helen Inglis. 4d.

BRIGHT.—Eighteen Sermons of S. Leo the Great on the Incarnation, translated with Notes and with the "Tome" of S. Leo in the original, by the Rev. W. Bright, D.D. 8vo., cloth, 5s.

BROWNE.—A Lecture on Symbolism and its Connection with Church Art, Architecture, &c. By C. Browne, Esq., M.A., late Scholar of Worcester College, Oxford. 3rd edition, with 22 Illustrations, and Appendix on the Symbolism of the Ecclesiastical Vestments. 1s. 6d.

BRETT, Mr. B.

The Churchman's Guide to Faith and Piety. A Manual of Instructions and Devotions.
Fourth Edition. Cloth, 3s. 6d.; antique calf or plain morocco, 8s. 3 vols. cloth,
4s.; limp calf, 11s; limp morocco, 12s.

Offices for the Sick and Dying. Reprinted from the above. 1s.

Leaflets for the Sick and Dying; supplementary to the Offices for the same in "The
Churchman's Guide to Faith and Piety." First Series. Price per set of eight.
6d.; cardboard, 9d.

A Guide to Confirmation. 8d.

The Christian's Daily Guide; or, Parochial Manual of Instruction and Devotion.
Part I. Faith and Duty, 3d.; II. Morning and Evening Prayers, 4d.; III. Prayers
during the day, and Collects for Particular Graces and Persons, 3d.; IV. Christian
Seasons.

Scripture History for the Young. Old and New Testaments. 9s. 6d., or with 16 engravings, 4s. 6d.

Devotions for the Sick Room, Prayers in Sickness, &c. Cloth, 9s. 6d.

Companion for the Sick Room; being a Compendium of Christian Doctrine. 2s. 6d.
These two bound together in 1 vol. cloth, price 5s.

A Pocket Companion for Lent, for Busy Men. In Two Parts. Price 2d.

A Manual of Devotions for School-boys. Compiled from various sources, 6d.

Devout Prayers on the Life and Passion of the Lord Jesus, by which the faithful
soul may increase in the Love of God. 3d., cloth 1s.

Fervent Aspirations after Divine Love and Thanksgivings on the Passion. Part II.
of the above, cloth 6d., wrapper, 6d.

Instructions, Prayers, and Holy Aspirations for the Sick Room. 4d., cloth 6d.

Prayers for Little Children and Young Persons. 6d.; cloth, 6d. Part I. 3d., cloth 6d.;
Part II. 4d., cloth, 6d.

Reflections, Meditations, and Prayers, on the Holy Life and Passion of our Lord.
New edition, 1s.

The Doctrine of the Cross, a Memorial of a Humble Follower of Christ. 1s.

A Few Practical Suggestions for the Burial of the Dead in Centre. With Two Plates. 4d.

BROWNLOW, The Rev. W. B.

Jesus, the Good Shepherd. A Short Memoir of Mellve H. M. Brownlow. New
edition. Cloth, with Sermon and Portrait, 2s. 6d. Cheap edition, 1s.

Lectures on the History of the Church of God, A.D. 31—161. 2s.

BUTLER, The Rev. W. J.

Sermons for Working Men in Country Parishes. Bold Type, 6s. 6d.

Twelve Short and Simple Meditations on the Sufferings of our Lord Jesus Christ.
Edited by the Rev. W. J. Butler. 1s. 6d.

Short Rules for Prayer for Working Men. 2d.

CANTICLES in the Morning and Evening Services, pointed correctly for Chanting,
1d., cloth 4d. With Chants 4d., cloth 6d.

CANTICLES in the Morning and Evening Services, arranged in Columns for Chanting. 2d.; limp cloth, 4d.

CANTICLES with blank staves for Chants. 2d.; cloth 4d.

CARTER, The Rev. T. T.

The Doctrine of the Priesthood in the Church of England. 4th Edition, 4s.

The Doctrine of Confession in the Church of England. Post 8vo., 6s.

Sermons. Vol. I. 3rd edition. 8vo., 14s. 6d.

Spiritual Instructions on the Holy Eucharist. Crown 8vo. 3rd edition, 2s. 6d.

Lent Lectures. 8vo., cloth, 9s.

1. The Imitation of our Lord. 5th edition. 2s. 6d.
2. The Passion and Temptation of our Lord. 2nd edition. 3s.
3. The Life of Sacrifice. 2nd edition. 2s. 6d.
4. The Life of Penitence. 2nd edition. 2s. 6d.

Family Prayers. 3rd edition. Cloth, 1s.

The Doctrine of the Holy Eucharist drawn from the Holy Scripture and the Records
of the Church. 3rd edition. Fcap. 8vo., 9d.

EDITED BY THE REV. T. T. CARTER.

A Book of Private Prayer for Morning, Mid-day, Night and other times, with Rules
for those who would live to God amid the business of daily life. 10th edition,
limp cloth, 1s.; cloth, red edges, 1s. 3d.; roan, 1s. 6d.; calf, 2s. 6d.

Litanies and other Devotions. 1s. 6d.

Night Offices for the Holy Week. 8vo., 2s. 6d.

CARTER, The Rev. T. T., Edited by
The Footprints of the Lord on the King's Highway of the Cross. Devotional Aids for Holy Week. Fcap. 8vo., cloth, 1s.
Footsteps of the Holy Child, being Readings on the Incarnation. Part I. 1s. Part II., 2s. 6d. In 1 vol. 4s. 6d. cloth.
Manual of Devotion for Sisters of Mercy. Part I. Prayers for Daily Use. 1s. 6d. Part II. For Different Necessities. 1s. Part III. For Forgiveness of Sins. 1s. Part IV. On the Holy Communion. 1s. Part V. Acts of Adoration, Faith, Hope, Love, &c. 1s. Part VI. Prayers to our Lord Jesus Christ, 1s. Part VII. Devotions on the Passion of our Lord Jesus Christ. 1s. Part VIII. Devotions for the Sick. 1s. 6d. In 2 volumes, cloth, 10s.; calf, 15s.
Short Office of the Holy Ghost. 1s.

CARTER.—Remarks on Christian Gravestones, with numerous Working Drawings, with Scales. By the Rev. Arthur J. Carter, M.A. 2nd edit. 2s. 6d.; stiff wrapper, 2s. 6d.

CATECHISM treating of the Unity of the Church, its Ministry, Liturgy, Offices, and Articles. By a Country Curate. 3d.

CATECHISM OF THEOLOGY. 18mo., cloth, 1s. 6d.; wrapper, 1s.

CATECHISM OF THE CHIEF THINGS WHICH A CHRISTIAN OUGHT TO KNOW AND BELIEVE TO HIS SOUL'S HEALTH. Edited by several Clergymen. New edition. 3d.

CHAMBERS, J. D.
The Doctrine of the Holy Eucharist, as Expounded by Herbert Thorndike, D.D. With a Preface by J. D. Chambers, M.A. 1s. 6d.
Lauda Syon. Ancient Latin Hymns of the English and other Churches, translated into corresponding metres. Fcp. 8vo. 5s.

CHAMBERS.—Fifty-two Sermons preached at Perth and other parts of Scotland. By the Rev. J. C. Chambers. Demy 8vo. 10s.

CHAMBERLAIN, The Rev. T.
The Theory of Christian Worship. Second Edition. 3s. 6d.
The Epistle to the Romans. With Short Notes, chiefly Critical and Doctrinal. Fcap. 8vo., cloth, 2s.
The Seven Ages of the Church, as indicated in the messages to the Seven Churches of Asia. Post 8vo., 2s.
English Grammar, and how to Teach it; together with a Lesson in Reading and Spelling. 3rd edit., 3d.
Hymns, chiefly for the Minor Festivals. 18mo., cloth, 1s.; wrapper 6d.

CHANTER, The Rev. J. M.
Sermons. 3s. 6d.
Help to an Exposition of the Catechism of the English Church. 6d.

CHAPTERS ON THE TE DEUM. By the Author of "Earth's many Voices." 18mo., cloth, 2s.

CHARITY AT HOME. A Tale. By the author of "Ruth Levison." 18mo. 2s.

CHEYNE, The Rev. P.
The Teaching of the Christian Year: a series of Sermons. Vol. I., Advent to Whitsuntide. 7s.
The Commixtions of the Cross. Fcap. 8vo., 2s.

CHILD'S GUIDE TO HOLINESS, The. Edited by a Priest. 18mo., wrapper 4d., cloth 6d.

CHILD'S NEW LESSON BOOK, or Stories for Little Readers. 1s.; 1s. 6d. cloth; coloured 2s. 6d.

CHORISTER BROTHERS, The. A Tale. By the Author of "The Children of the Chapel." &c. 3rd edition. Fcap. 8vo., 4s.

CHRIST IN THE LAW; or, the Gospel Foreshadowed in the Pentateuch. Compiled from various sources. By a Priest of the Church of England. Fcap. 8vo., cloth, 2s. 6d.

CHRIST IN THE PROPHETS: Joshua, Judges, Samuel, Kings. Fcap. 8vo., 2s. 6d.

CHRISTIAN CHILDREN, Scenes in the Lives of; with Questions on separate cards. The Cards enclosed in a case. 2s.

CHRISTIAN DUTIES, as essentially conducive to progress in the Spiritual Life. 2nd Edition. 3s. 6d.

CHRISTIAN SERVANT (The) taught from the Catechism her Faith and Practice. By the Author of the "Servants' Hall." Edited by the Rev. Sir W. H. Cope, Bart. Fcap. 8vo., cloth.   (Pub. 7s.) *Reduced to 3s.*

CHRISTIAN SERVANT'S BOOK of Devotion, Self-Examination, and Advice. Sixth edition, cloth 1s.

CHRISTIAN WEEK, The, a Manual of Devotion with Psalms and Hymns for Schools and Families. 6d.

A CHRISTMAS PRESENT for Children. From the German. 1s.

CHRONICLES OF S. MARY'S. By S. D. N. Crown 8vo., 6s.

CHURCH FLORAL DECORATION, Practical Hints on. With twenty plates. Fourth Edition. 2s. plain; 3s. 6d. coloured.

CHURCH CATECHISM, The.—Printed on tinted paper, with seventeen engravings drawn by Gilbert. Price 1s. cloth. A cheap edition, 6d.

CHURCH DOCTRINES PROVED BY THE BIBLE. Fcap. 8vo., 1s.

CHURCH OF ENGLAND MINISTERS. How they are made, and what they are. 4d.

CHURCHMAN'S COMPANION. A Monthly Magazine, 6d. Vols. I. to XL. 7s. each.
Second Series. Vols. I. to VI. 4s. each.
Third Series, enlarged. Vols. I. to VIII. 4s. each.

CHURCHMAN'S DIARY; an Almanack and Directory for the Celebration of the Service of the Church. Published annually. 4d.; interleaved, 6d.; cloth, 1s. 6d.; roan tuck, 2s.

THE CHURCHMAN'S LIBRARY.

The *Churchman's Library* consists of Tracts and Manuals; of the former there are twelve published, price 2s.

1. Sunday; and how to spend it. 2d.
2. Catholic and Protestant. 2d.
3. Grace; and how to gain it. 2d.
4. Church Worship. 2d.
5. The Prayer Book; and how to use it. 2d.
6. The Heavenly Lives of the Primitive Christians. 2d.
7. Holy Scripture; and how to use it. 2d.
8. All Christians, Priests. 2d.
9. The Threefold Work of Cnrist. 2d.
10. The Doctrine of Justification. 2d.
11. The Priest and the People. 2d.
12. Outlines of Christian Doctrine. 2d.
The above in a packet, price 2s.

The Manuals published are:—
1. Questions and Answers Illustrative of the Church Catechism. 4d.; cloth, 6d.
2. Bishop Andrewes' Devotions. 6d.; cloth 1s.; calf or morocco 3s. 6d.
3. The Laying on of Hands; a Manual for Confirmation. 4d.; cloth, 6d.
4. Guide to the Eucharist. Containing Instructions and Directions with Forms of Preparation and Self-Examination. 4d.
5. The Manual; a Book of Devotion, chiefly intended for the Poor. 17th Edition. Limp cloth, 1s.; cloth boards, rededged, 1s. 6d.; leather, 1s. 6d.; cheap edition, 3d.

CLARKE.—The Watch-Tower Book; or, Readings for the Night Watches of Advent. By the Rev. C. W. B. Clarke, M.A. Post 8vo., cloth boards, 3s. 6d.; limp cloth, 2s.

CLEAVER, Rev. W. H.
Five Plain Sermons on the Sacrament of the Altar. Preached at the Church of S. Mary Magdalene, Paddington. With a Supplementary Sermon on "Confession." By the Rev. W. H. Cleaver, Assistant Priest. Third edition. Fcap. 8vo., 1s.
Short Devotions for the Sacrament of the Altar. Second Edition. 4d.

CLERGYMAN'S (The) **MANUAL OF PRIVATE PRAYERS.** Collected and Compiled from Various Sources. A Companion Book to the "Priest's Prayer Book." Cloth, 1s.

CODE.—Sermons addressed to a Country Congregation, including Four preached as Select Preacher before the University of Cambridge, in January, 1864. With a Few Thoughts in Verse. By the Rev. E. T. Codd. Third Series. 12mo., cloth, 6s. 6d.

COLLECTS from the Book of Common Prayer. 32mo. sewed 2d., rubricated, and in parchment cover, 4d.

COLLECTS EXPLAINED IN A CATECHETICAL FORM. Part I. 4d. Part II., 3d.

COMPANION TO THE SUNDAY SERVICES of the Church of England. 2s. 6d.

CONFIRMATION CERTIFICATES, &c.

A Memorial of Baptism, Confirmation, and Holy Communion. On card, printed in gold and colours, with cunire cross and scroll. 1d.

Certificate of Baptism, Confirmation, and First Communion, on a card printed in red and blue, 2d., or 14s. per 100.

Certificates of Confirmation and Holy Communion. On a card, printed in red and black, price 1d. each, or 7s. per 100. On an Ornamented large card, 3d.; also new design, 2d.

A Confirmation Medal of appropriate Design. 6d.

Card of Admission to Confirmation. 7s. 6d. per 100.

CONFRATERNITY OF THE BLESSED SACRAMENT PUBLICATIONS.

The MANUAL OF THE CONFRATERNITY. Fourth edition, revised and enlarged, 4d.; cloth, red edges, 6d.

An ALTAR BOOK FOR YOUNG PERSONS. Suitable also for Choristers. Cloth, with a picture of the Crucifixion, &c., with 5 pictures, 1s. 3d.; do. red edges, gold lettered, 1s. 6d.

CONVERSATIONS WITH COUSIN RACHEL. Complete in One Vol. 2s. 6d.

COSIN, Bishop.
A Collection of Private Devotions for the Hours of Prayer. 1s.; calf, 2s. 6d.
The Sum of the Catholic Faith, from Bishop Cosin. 2d., or 14s. per 100.

COTTAGE COMMENTARY.—Vol. I.: S. Matthew, limp cloth, 2s. 6d.; cloth boards, 3s. Vol. II.: S. Mark, limp cloth, 1s. 6d.; cloth boards, 2s. Vol. III.: S. Luke, 2s. 6d. Vol. IV.: S. John, limp cloth, 2s. 6d.; cloth boards, 3s.; calf, 7s. Vol. V.: The Epistles to the Hebrews, S. James, S. Peter, S. John, and S. Jude. 2s. 6d. The Four Gospels, in Two vols., cloth, 8s. 6d.

COUPER.—A Few Hints to Mothers on the Management of Children, &c. By Georgina Couper. Dedicated to the Very Rev. and Hon. the Dean of Windsor. Demy 12mo., 2d.

CRANBORNE, Viscount.—A History of France for Children, in a Series of Letters. By the late Viscount Cranborne. 2s. 6d.

CUDLIP.—A Noble Aim. By Annie Thomas, (Mrs. Pender Cudlip.) Published for the Benefit of the Devon Home of Mercy. Fcap. 8vo., 1s.

DAILY EVENTS OF HOLY WEEK. Written in Plain Words. Fcap. 8vo., 6d.; cloth, 1s.

DAILY LIFE OF THE CHRISTIAN CHILD. A poem for children. 3d. Cheap edition, in book or on sheet, 1d.; mounted on board, 6d.

DAKEYNE.—The Sword and the Cross. By the Rev. J. O. Dakeyne, M.A. 2s. 6d.

DAVIDSON.—The Holy Communion. A Course of Sermons preached in the Parish Church of Chipping Sodbury. By J. F. F. Davidson, M.A. Vicar. Fcap. 8vo., 3s. 6d.

DAVIES.—Benefit Club Sermons. 1st and 2nd Series. In One Vol. By the Rev. G. Davies. Second edition. 4to., 3s.

DAY HOURS OF THE CHURCH OF ENGLAND, newly Translated and Arranged according to the Prayer Book and the Authorised Translation of the Bible. 3rd edition. Crown 8vo., wrapper, 1s.; cloth, 1s. 6d.; limp calf or morocco, 7s.

DAY OFFICE OF THE CHURCH, (The) according to the Kalendar of the Church of England; consisting of Lauds, Vespers, Prime, Terce, Sext, None, and Compline, throughout the Year. To which are added, the Order for the Administration of the Reserved Eucharist, Penance, and Unction; together with the Office of the Dead, Commendation of a Soul, divers Benedictions and Offices, and full Rubrical Directions.

A complete Edition, especially for Sisterhoods and Religious Houses. By the Editor of "The Little Hours of the Day." Crown 8vo., 4s. 6d.; cloth, red edges, 5s. 6d.; calf, 9s. 6d.; morocco, 10s. 6d.

DENISON.—Sarum on the Holy Eucharist. The Original Latin from a MS. in the British Museum hitherto unpublished. The Translation by the Archdeacon of Taunton. Demy 8vo, 7s. 6d.

DEVOTIONS FOR HOLY COMMUNION. 32mo., cloth, 1s.

DEVOTIONAL AIDS FOR THE USE OF THE CLERGY. 32mo. parchment, 1s.

DIAL OF MEDITATION AND PRAYER. 2nd edition, 3d.

DICKINSON.—List of Service Books according to the Uses of the Anglican Church, with the possessors. 1s. 6d.

DISTRICT VISITOR'S MEMORANDUM BOOK. 8d., the paper in. per quire.

DIVINE MASTER, The: a Devotional Manual illustrating the Way of the Cross. With Ten Steel Engravings. 9th edition, 3s. 6d.; morocco 5s.; antique calf or morocco 7s. Cheap edition in wrapper, 1s.
The Engravings separately on a sheet, 9d.

DOMESTIC OFFICES; being Morning and Evening Prayer for the Use of Families. Wrapper, 6d.; cloth, 8d.

DOUGLAS.—Mary and Mildred; or, Principle the Guide of Impulse. Edited by the Rev. Mair Douglas. 2nd edition. 5s.

DROP IN THE OCEAN, or the Little Wreath of Fancy. By Agnes and Bessie. 2nd edition. 1s.

DUKE.—Systematic Analysis of Bishop Butler's Analogy. By the Rev. Henry M. Duke, B.A. 3s. 6d., interleaved 5s.

EARNEST APPEAL ON BEHALF OF PUBLIC WORSHIP. Extracted from Bp. Patrick's Discourse concerning Prayer. 1s.

EASY LESSONS FOR THE YOUNGER CHILDREN IN SUNDAY SCHOOLS. By the Author of "Conversations with Cousin Rachel." 6d. Questions, for the Use of the Teacher. 6d.

EASY CATECHISM OF THE OLD TESTAMENT HISTORY, with the dates of the principal events. 18mo. Third Edition. 8d.

ECCLES.—Midsummer Holidays at Princes Green. By Mrs. Eccles, author of "The Riches of Poverty." 18mo., 1s.

ECCLESIOLOGIST, The. Published under the Superintendence of the Ecclesiological Society.
The First Series, 5 Vols. in 1, and the New Series, 26 Vols. cloth, are now offered at the reduced price of £5. 5s. for the set.

ECCLESIOLOGY, Hand-Book of English. Companion for Church Tourists. Cloth, 2s. 6d.

ECHOES OF OUR CHILDHOOD. By the author of "Everley," &c. Fcap. 4to., toned paper, with illustrations, 2s. 6d.

EDMONSTONE, Sir Archibald, Bart.
Portions of the Psalms, selected and arranged for Devotional Purposes. Paper 6d.; cloth, 10d.
The Christian Gentleman's Daily Walk. 2s. 6d.

EIGENWILLIG; or, the Self-Willed. A Fairy Extravaganza. A Dramatic Version of "The Hope of the Katzekopfs." Crown 8vo., 6d.

EIGHTY-FOURTH PSALM, Treatise on the. By the late Lady Harriet Howard. 32mo., cl. 6d., bound, 1s.

ELLIS.—From the Font to the Altar: a Manual of Christian Doctrine for the Young, especially those who are preparing for Confirmation. By the Rev. Coonyngham Ellis, Second Edition. 1s. 6d. cloth; 1s. wrapper.

EMBROIDERY, Ecclesiastical. Working Patterns of Flowers on sheets, Nos. 1 to 10, 6d. each, or in Three Parts, 2s. each.

EMBROIDERY, (Church.) A New Practical Hints on. With Six Plates, 1s.

ENGLISH CATHOLIC'S DAILY TEXT BOOK. By the Editor of the "English Catholic's Devotions for the Stations," &c. 18mo., cl. 2d.; interleaved, 2s. 6d.

ERRINGTON.—Prayers for Soldiers, by Colonel Errington. 3d.

EUCHARISTIC DEVOTIONS, with Preparations and Thanksgivings for Young Persons Unconfirmed or not Communicating. Royal 32mo., cloth, 9d. A companion book to "The Devout Chorister," and may be had bound with it, 1s. 6d. cl.

EUCHARISTIC MONTH: being short Daily Preparation and Thanksgiving for the Holy Communion. 2d.; cloth 1s.; bound 1s. 6d.

EVANS, The late Archdeacon R. W.
Tales of the Ancient British Church. Cloth 2s. 6d.
Daily Hymns. 3s. 6d.

EVANS.—Christianity in its Homely Aspects: Sermons on Various Subjects, delivered in the Church of S. Andrew, Wells Street, and elsewhere. By the Rev. A. B. Evans, D.D. Second Series. 3s.

EVANS.—Pietas Puerilis; or, Childhood's Path to Heaven, and other Poems. Dedicated by special permission to H. R. H. the Duchess of Cambridge. By the Rev. A. B. Evans. 8vo., board paper, 3s. 6d.

EVERLEY. A Tale. Second Edition. fcap. 8vo. 6s.

EVENING MEETINGS, The; or, the Pastor among the Boys of his Flock. By C. M. S. Reprinted from the Churchman's Companion. fcap. 8vo., 6s.

EXPLANATION OF SOME SCRIPTURAL AND ECCLESIASTICAL TERMS. 3rd edition, 3d.

FAMILY PRAYERS for the Children of the Church. 4d., cloth 6d.

FANNY'S FLOWERS; or, Fun for the Nursery. With several engravings. 1s.; cloth gilt, 1s. 6d.

FASTS AND FESTIVALS OF THE CHURCH, in a conversational form. 1s. 6d.

A FEW DEVOTIONAL HELPS FOR THE CHRISTIAN SEASONS.
Royal 32mo. 3 Vols., cloth 4s. 6d.
Advent, Christmas, and the Seasons until Lent (196 pp.) 1s.
Lent and Passion-tide (93 pp.) 6d.
Easter-tide (48 pp.) 4d.
From Rogation to Trinity (136 pp.) 6d.
The Saints' Days (135 pp.) 8d.
Trinity. Part I. 1s. 4d.
Trinity. Part II. 1s.

A FEW WORDS TO LITTLE CHILDREN ABOUT THE SEASONS OF THE CHRISTIAN YEAR. By C. E. F. 4d.

A FEW WORDS TO A CHRISTIAN MOURNER. 2d.

FIVE TALES OF OLD TIME. Separately in cloth, 6d. each. Follow Me. (C. E. H., Morwenstow.)—The Shepherd of the Giant Mountains. (Fouqué.)—The Knight and the Enchantress. (Fouqué.)

FLOWER, The late Rev. W. B.
Sermons for the Seasons of the Church, translated from S. Bernard. 8vo. 6s.
The Three Books of Theophilus to Autolycus on the Christian Religion. Translated, with Notes. 3s. 6d.
Classical Tales and Legends. 5s., cheap edition 1s.
Tales of Faith and Providence. 3s.
The Widow and her Son; with other Tales. Translated from the German. 18mo., cloth, 2s.

FORBES.—Snowball and other Tales. By Isabella Forbes. 2s. 6d.

FORD, The Rev. J.
Twelve Sermons from the Quaresimale of P. Paolo Segneri, 2nd edition. 6s.
A Second Series of Twelve Sermons from the same. 6s.
A Third Series of Twelve Sermons from the same. 6s.
     The Three Series in one vol., cloth, 14s.
Twelve Sermons, preached in the Chapel of Liverydole Almshouse, at Heavitree.
     12mo., cloth, 5s.
Thoughts in Verse on Private Prayer and Public Worship. 1s. 6d.
The Gospel of S. Matthew Illustrated from Ancient and Modern Authors, chiefly in
     the Doctrinal and Moral Sense. 2nd edition. 11s.
The Gospel of S. Mark Illustrated. 2nd edition. 10s.
The Gospel of S. Luke Illustrated. 2nd edition. 19s.
The Gospel of S. John Illustrated. 2nd edition. 10s.
The Acts of the Apostles. 12s.
S. Paul's Epistle to the Romans. 12s.

**FORM OF PRAYER AND CEREMONIES USED AT THE CONSE-
CRATION OF CHURCHES,** &c., in London and Winchester. 1d., or 7s.
per 100. Form for Oxford Diocese. 2d., or 14s. per 100.

**FORM OF PRAYER FOR LAYING THE STONE OF A CHURCH
OR CHAPEL.** 1d.

FORM OF PRAYER FOR LAYING THE STONE OF A SCHOOL.
2s. 6d. per 100.

FORM OF PRAYER FOR OPENING A NEW SCHOOL. 2s. 6d. per 100.

FORM OF SELF-EXAMINATION; with Prayers Preparatory to the Holy
Communion. 2d.

**FORM OF SERVICE FOR CONSECRATING CEMETERY CHA-
PELS.** [Rochester Diocese.] 7s. per 100.

FORSYTH'S BOOK OF NEW MONUMENTAL DESIGNS, with an
Introduction by the Rev. Charles Boutell, M.A. 4to. 2nd edition, 10s. 6d.

FOWLE.—The Epistle to the Hebrews the Epistle of S. Paul. By the Rev. W. H.
Fowle. 1s. 6d.

FOX, The Rev. S.
The Noble Army of Martyrs. 2s.; cheap edition, 1s.
The Holy Church throughout all the world. 2s., cheap edition, 1s.

FREDERICK GORDON, or the Storming of the Redan. By a Soldier's Daughter.
Royal 18mo., 1s.

FREEMAN.—History of Architecture. By E. A. Freeman. (Pub. 14s.) Reduced to 8s.

FREEMAN.—Four Sermons for the Season of Advent. By the Ven. Archdeacon
Freeman. Post 8vo., 2s.

GALTON, The Rev. J. L.
Notes of Lectures on the Book of Canticles or Song of Solomon, delivered in the
     Parish Church of S. Sidwell, Exeter. 6s.
One Hundred and Forty-two Lectures on the Book of Revelation. In Two Vols. 10s.

GERTRUDE DACRE. By the author of "The Sunbeam." 2s.

GOD'S CHURCH ON EARTH. Fcap. 8vo. 6d.

GOING HOME. A Story. By F. G. W. 3rd ed. 1s. 6d. cloth.

GOODRICH.—Claudie; the Days of Martyrdom. A Tale. By A. M. Goodrich.
Fcap. 8vo. cloth, 2s. 6d.

GOOD SAYINGS FOR EVERY DAY OF THE YEAR. 6d.

GOODWIN.—A Short Account of the Art of Polychrome, Historical and Practical.
By T. Goodwin, B.A. 1s. 6d.

GRANDFATHER'S CHRISTMAS STORY, The. With Illustration and
ornamental borders. 6d.

GRAY.—The Christian's Plain Guide. By the Rev. Walter A. Gray, M.A., Vicar of
Arlesey. 32mo., cloth 1d.; wrapper, 6d.

GRANTHAM, The Rev. G. P.
"Name this Child;" or a Few Words to Parents and Sponsors concerning the Selection of Suitable and Correct Names for Children. By the Rev. G. P. Grantham. 6d.
The Mysteries of Holy Church, and other Verses. 2s. 6d.

GREAT TRUTHS OF THE CHRISTIAN RELIGION. Edited by the Rev. W. U. Richards. Fourth edition. 2s. cloth; or in five parts, wrappers, 2s. 6d.

GRESLEY, The Rev. W.
Priests and Philosophers. Foap. 8vo., 2s. 6d.
Practical Sermons. 2s. 6d.
Sermons preached at Brighton. 2s. 6d.
Sophron and Neologus, or Common Sense Philosophy. 2s.
Treatise on the English Church; containing Remarks on its History, Theory, &c. 1s.
An Essay on Confession, Penance, and Absolution. By Mr. Roger Laurence, with a Preface by the Rev. W. Gresley. 1s.
The Present State of the Controversy with Rome. Three Sermons preached in St. Paul's, Brighton.
The Forest of Arden, a Tale of the English Reformation. 3s.; cheap edition, 2s.
The Siege of Lichfield, a Tale of the Great Rebellion. 4s.; cheap edition, 1s. 6d.
Common Hall; or, the Jacobites: A Tale of the Revolution of 1688. 2s.
Charles Lever; the Man of the Nineteenth Century. 2s.; cheap edition, 1s. 6d.
Clement Walton; or, the English Citizen. 3s.; cheap edition, 1s. 6d.
Frank's First Trip to the Continent. 3s.
Bernard Leslie, a Tale of the Times. (1838.) 2s.
Bernard Leslie, Second Part, 3s.
Holiday Tales. 1s., wrapper 1s. 6d.
Portrait of an English Churchman. 9th edition, 2s. 6d.

HACKET.—An Account of the Life and Death of the Right Rev. Father in God, John Hacket, late Lord Bishop of Lichfield and Coventry. Published by Thomas Plume, D.D., and edited with large additions and copious Notes, by Mackenzie E. C. Walcott, B.D. Fcap. 8vo., 2s. 6d.

HALLAM.—Monumental Memorials; being Designs for Headstones and Mural Monuments. By J. W. Hallam, Architect. imp. 8vo. Parts I. and II., 3s. 6d. each.

HAMILTON.—Parochial Sermons. By the Rev. L. R. Hamilton. Fcap. 8vo., 3s. 6d.

HANCOCK.—The Children of Rose Lynn. By Selina Hancock. 18mo., 1s.

HAWKER.—Echoes from Old Cornwall. By the Rev. R. S. Hawker, M.A. 3s. 6d.

HELMORE, Frederick, Esq.
Church Choirs; containing Directions for the Formation, Management, and Instruction of Cathedral, Collegiate, and Parochial Choirs; being the result of twenty-two years' experience in Choir Training. 3rd edition. 1s.
Eighty Short Exercises, in Eight Lessons, on the Major Scale. 6d.
The Chorister's Instruction Book. The result of thirty years' practical experience in all the more popular methods of teaching the Rudiments of Music. Crown 8vo., 2d.

HELPS FOR CONFIRMATION AND FIRST COMMUNION. By Two Priests of the Church of England. 6d.

HENRIETTA'S WISH. A Tale. By the author of "The Heir of Redclyffe." Fourth Edition. 3s.

HEYGATE, The Rev. W. E.
The Manual; a Book of Devotion. Seventeenth edition. Cloth, limp, 1s.; boards, 1s. 3d.; roan, 1s. 6d.; cheap edition. 6d.
The Manual. Adapted for general use. 12mo., cloth, 1s. 6d.
The Evening of Life; or Meditations and Devotions for the Aged. Post 8vo., large type. 3s. 6d.
Ember Hours. New edition revised, with an Essay on Religion in Relation to Science, by the Rev. T. S. Ackland, M.A., Vicar of Puleo, author of "Story of Creation," &c. Fcap. 8vo., cloth, 3s.
Catholic Antidotes. Post 8vo. 5s. 6d.
William Blake; or, the English Farmer. 3s. 6d.
Godfrey Davenant at School. 3s.
Ellen Meyrick; or, False Examples. 2d.
Memoir of the Rev. John Aubone Cook, M.A., Vicar of South Benfleet and Rural Dean, Essex. cloth. 1s.
The Wedding Gift. A Devotional Manual for the Married, or those intending to Marry. 2nd edition, revised and enlarged. 2s.

HICKS.—Catechetical Lectures on the Incarnation. By the Rev. James Hicks. **2s.**

HICKS.—General View of the Doctrine of Baptismal Regeneration. By the Rev. W. H. Hicks. **9d.**

HIDDEN LIFE, The. Translated from Nouvon's Pensées Chrétiennes. 3rd edition, enlarged. 18mo., **3s.**

HIERURGIA ANGLICANA; or Documents and Extracts Illustrative of the Ritual of the Church of England after the Reformation. 8vo., cloth, with Illustrations, 13s.

HIGHER CLAIMS; or, Catharine Lewis the Sunday School Teacher. Edited by the Rev. R. Seymour, M.A. 18mo., cloth, 1s.

HILARY S. MAGNA; or, the Nearest Duty first. A Tale. Fcap. 8vo., 4s.

HILL.—Short Sermons on some leading Principles of Christian Life. By the Rev. R. Hill. 6s.

HILL.—Stories on the Commandments. The First Table: "My duty towards God." By the Rev. G. Hill. 1s. cloth, or in a packet.

HINTS ON EARLY EDUCATION, addressed to Mothers. By a Mother. 2nd edition. Edited by the Archbishop of Dublin. 6d.

HOLIDAYS AT S. MARY'S; or, Tales in a Sisterhood. By S. D. N., author of "Chronicles of S. Mary's." 18mo., cloth, 2s. 6d.

HOLY CHILD JESUS. Thoughts and Prayers on the Holy Infancy and Childhood of our Blessed Lord and Saviour, Jesus Christ. With 4 Engravings. 1s. 6d. cloth; 1s. wrapper; morocco, 4s.

HOLY CHILDHOOD OF OUR BLESSED LORD. Meditations for a Month. By the Author of "Tales of Kirkbeck." 6d.

HOLY EUCHARIST, The. A Manual containing Directions and suitable Devotions for those who remain in Church but do not Communicate. By a Parish Priest. 6d.

HOME FOR CHRISTMAS. 18mo., 1s. 6d.

HOPKINS.—Plena Metrica. By the Rev. T. M. Hopkins. 2s. 6d.

HOPKINS.—The Law of Ritualism, examined in its Relation to the Word of God, to the Primitive Church, to the Church of England, and to the Protestant Episcopal Church in the United States. By the late Right Rev. John Henry Hopkins, D.D., Bishop of Vermont. Second Edition. 2s. A Reprint of the above, for distribution, in fcap. 8vo., 1s.

HOPWOOD, The late Rev. H.
School Geography. New edition. 2s.; cheap edition, 1s.
The Child's Geography, being an abridgment of the above. 1s.

HOROLOGY; or Dial of Prayer, for the pocket. 1s.

HOSMER.—Hearing Mass and other customs considered. By the Rev. A. H. Hosmer, 8vo., 2s. 6d.

HOUSMAN.—Readings on the Psalms, with Notes on their Musical Treatment, originally addressed to Choristers. By the Rev. H. Housman, late Chaplain of Bareculum. Fcap. 8vo., cloth, 3s. 6d.

HOW TO COME TO CHRIST. By the Author of "Our New Life in Christ." Fcap. 8vo, 6d.

HUBERT NEVILLE. A Tale. By the Author of "The Neglected Opportunity," &c. Fcap. 8vo. 2s.

HUGHES.—Tracts for Parish Distribution. By the late Rev. E. J. H. Hughes. Six in a packet, 3d.

HUSBAND.—Truths of the Catholic Religion. Being Short Extracts from Sermons, preached in S. Mary's Church, Atherstone. By the Rev. Edward Husband. 6d.

HUTCHINGS, The Rev. W. H.
The Person and Work of the Holy Ghost. A Series of Lectures delivered in substance at All Saints', Margaret Street, in Lent, 1866. By the Rev. W. H. Hutchings, M.A., Subwarden of the House of Mercy, Clewer. 8vo., 3s.
Some Aspects of the Cross. Seven Discourses delivered in S. Andrew's, Clewer. Crown 8vo., cloth, 4s.

HYDE.—The Catechism of the Church of England, with analysis, notes, explanations, and illustrations from the Holy Scriptures, for the use of Children. By T. J. Hyde. 4d.

HYMNS AND INTROITS, with some Anthems, adapted to the Seasons of the Christian Year. Strongly bound in cloth, 8d.; limp cloth, 6d.; roan, 1s. 3d.

HYMNS OF THE HOLY FEAST. Square 24mo., on tinted paper, and rubricated, 6d.

HYMNS FOR INFANT CHILDREN. 32mo., 1d. With MUSIC, edited by the Rev. J. B. Dykes, M.A., Mus. Doc. 1s.

INCARNATION, The. A Series of Tracts on the connection of Church Principles with the Incarnation.
No. 1. The Incarnation. 2d.
No. 2. The Incarnation; Christ and His Sacraments. 2d.

INCARNATION, Catechism on the. Founded on Bishop Bull's "State of Man before the Fall," &c. 1s.

INNES.—Five Sermons preached in Advent and on the Festival of the Holy Innocents, in the Parish Church of Downe, Kent. By the Rev. John Innes, M.A., 1s. 6d.

INTERMEDIATE STATE, The. A Poem dedicated (with permission from himself, to the late Author of the "Christian Year." Fcap. 8vo., cloth, 1s. 3d.

ION LESTER. A Tale, by C. H. H. Fcp. 8vo., 4s. 6d.

IRONS, The Rev. W. J.
The Judgments on Baptismal Regeneration; with Appendices, and a Discourse on Heresy. 3s. 6d.
On the Whole Doctrine of Final Causes: a Dissertation, with a Chapter on Modern Deism. 7s. 6d.
On the Holy Catholic Church, as a Witness against False Philosophising. 4s. 6d.
Ecclesiastical Jurisdiction: being Four Lectures on The Synod—The Diocese—The Parish—The Priest. 7s. 6d.
The Preaching of Christ. A Series of Sixty Sermons for the People. In a pocket, 6s. Cloth, 6s.
The Miracles of Christ: being a Second Series of Sermons for the People. Second Edition. 8vo., cloth, 6s.
The Christian Servant's Book of Devotion, Self-Examination, and Advice. Sixth Edition. 17mo., cloth, 1s.

ISLAND CHOIR, or the Children of the Child Jesus. 4d.

IVO AND VERENA, or the Snowdrop; a Tale of the Early Christians. By the author of "Cousin Rachel." 1s.; limp cloth, 1s. 6d.

IVON. By the Author of "Aunt Agnes," and "Is he Clever?" Fcap. 8vo. 3s. 6d.

JENKINS.—Synchronistical or Contemporary Annals of the Kings and Prophets of Israel and Judah. By W. J. Jenkins, M.A. 4s.

JOHNS, C. A.—Examination Questions on the Pentateuch. For the Use of Schools. By the Rev. C. A. Johns, B.A., F.L.S. 1s.

JOHNS, The Rev. B. G.
The Collects and Catechising throughout the year. 2s.
Easy Dictation Lessons, original and selected. 6d.; cloth 8d.

JOHNSON.—Prayers and Meditations composed by Dr. Johnson. With a Preface by the Rev. W. Greeley, M.A. 18mo. cloth, 2s. 6d.

Juvenile Englishman's Historical Library.
Edited by the Rev. J. F. Russell, B.C.L.

English History for Children. By the Rev. J. M. Neale. 3s.; limp cloth, 1s. 6d.
History of Greece. Edited by the Rev. J. M. Neale. 2s.
History of Rome. By the Rev. Samuel Fox, M.A., F.S.A. 2s.
History of Spain. By the Rev. Bennett G. Johns. 2s.
History of Portugal. By the Rev. J. M. Neale. 2s.
History of Ireland. Edited by the late Rev. T. K. Arnold, B.D. 2s.
History of Scotland. By the Rev. W. B. Flower, B.A. 2s.
Cheap Editions, in limp cloth, 1s. each.

The Juvenile Englishman's Library.

The early Volumes were Edited by the Hon. F. E. Paget; the later by the Rev. J. F. Russell.

Tales of the Village Children. By the Rev. F. E. Paget. First Series, 2s.

The Hope of the Katzekopfs; a Fairy Tale. By the Rev. F. E. Paget. 2s.

Tales of the Village Children. By the Rev. F. E. Paget. Second Series, 2s.

The Triumphs of the Cross. Tales of Christian Heroism. By the Rev. J. M. Neale. 2s.

The Triumphs of the Cross. Part II. Tales of Christian Endurance. By the Rev. J. M. Neale. 2s.

The Charcoal Burners. 1s. 6d.

Godfrey Davenant; a Tale of School Life. By the Rev. W. E. Heygate. 2s.

Lake Sharp, or Knowledge without Religion. By the Rev. F. E. Paget. 2s.

School Geography, with a Chapter on the Ecclesiastical Geography of Great Britain. By the Rev. H. Hopwood. 2s.

Forninge; a Tale of the Revolution, 1688. 2s.

The Manger of the Holy Night, from the German. By C. E. H. Morwenstow. 2s.

Stories from Heathen Mythology. By the Rev. J. M. Neale. 3s.

Cheap Editions, in wrapper, 1s. each.

KALENDAR OF THE IMITATION: Sentences for every day in the year, from the Imitatio Christi. $2mo., cloth, 1s.

KEMPIS.—The Soliloquy of the Soul, and the Garden of Roses. Translated from Thomas à Kempis. By the Rev. W. H. Flower, M.A. 2s.; cheap edition, 1s.

KEN, Bishop,
Prayers for Morning and Evening. 3s. 6d. per 100.
Practice of Divine Love. 2s.; cheap edition, 9d.
Preparation for Death. 1s.

LAST SLEEP OF THE CHRISTIAN CHILD. A poem, companion to the "Daily Life." 3d.; or on a sheet, 1d.

LAURENCE.—The Churchman's Assistant at Holy Communion; being so much of the Order of Administration as is engaged with the actual celebration of that Sacrament. With Additions and Directions for the use of Communicants. By the Rev. Robert F. Laurence, M.A. Fcap. 8vo. cloth, 2s.

LAYING ON OF HANDS: A Manual for Confirmation, with Helps preparatory to receiving that Holy Ordinance. 4d., cloth 6d.

LEA, The Rev. W.
Catechisings on the Prayer Book. 3rd edition, 18mo. cloth, 1s.
Catechisings on the Life of our Lord. 18mo. cloth, 2s. 6d.
Sermons on the Prayer Book, preached at Rome. Fcap. 8vo. 2s.

LEE, The Rev. F. G.
The Message of Reconciliation. Four Advent Sermons. 8vo. 1s.
Miscellaneous Sermons, by Clergymen of the Church of England. Edited by the Rev. Frederick G. Lee, F.S.A. (Pub. 8s. 6d.) Reduced to 3s. 6d.

LEGENDA DOMESTICA: Lessons for the Sundays, Holy-days, and Week-days, throughout the Year. Selected for the Offices of Family Devotion, and arranged according to the Kalendar of the Church of England. 1s.

LESSONS FOR LITTLE CHILDREN ON THE SEASONS OF THE CHURCH. By C. A. E. 1s.

LESSONS FOR LITTLE CHILDREN FROM THE HISTORY OF THE CHURCH. By C. A. E. 1s.

LESSONS FOR EVERY DAY IN THE WEEK, with Hymns and Music. By the Author of "Conversations with Cousin Rachel." 3d. Companion to the Lessons, for the use of the Teacher. 1s.

LESSONS IN GRAMMAR FOR A CHILD. Large type, price 4d.

LESSONS ON THE CREED. What we are to believe. 1s. 6d.

LEVETT.—Gentle Influence; or, The Cousin's Visit. By F. M. Levett. Third Edition. 2s.

LITANY, The. Handsomely printed in red and black. For the Litany Desk.

LITANIES.
The Litany Appendix; containing a Mission Service, twenty Metrical Litanies and Metrical Hymns. 1d.; cloth, 6d.
Litany of our Lord. 1s. 6d. per 100.
Litany of the Name of Jesus. 12mo., 1d.
A Metrical Litany of Penitence (from the "People's Hymnal,") with a suitable Tune; for use in Church. 2s. 6d. per 100.
Litany of the Passion, with a suitable Tune. 2s. 6d. per 100.
Litany of Penitence and Litany of the Passion (from "The People's Hymnal.") The Music for Four Voices. By J. George, Organist of S. Mary Magdalene, Addlestone. 1d., or 3s. per 100.

LITTLEDALE.—Commentary on the Song of Songs. By the Rev. R. F. Littledale, LL.D., D.C.L. 12mo. antique cloth, 7s.

LITTLE HOURS OF THE DAY, according to the Kalendar of the Church of England. 3s. 6d. cloth; 2s. 6d. wrapper.

LITTLE ALICE AND HER SISTER. Edited by the Rev. W. Orraley. 6s.

LITURGIES.
Liturgy of S. John Chrysostom, translated from the Greek according to the Euchologion, and compared with the Slavonic. 2s.
Liturgy of S. John Chrysostom in Greek and English. 3s. 6d.
The Scottish Communion Office in Greek. Edited by the Bishop of Brechin. 3s. 6d., 2s.
The Liturgies of 1549 and 1604. Edited by the Rev. Orby Shipley, M.A. Fcap. 8vo. Cloth, 1s. 6d.
The Liturgy of King Edward VI., A.D. 1549. 3d.
Ordinary and Canon of the Mass, according to the Use of the Church of Sarum. Translated, with Introduction and Notes, by John Theodore Dodd, B.A., late Junior Student of Christ Church, Oxford. Fcap. 8vo., cloth, 1s. 6d.
The Penny Liturgy; containing the Service for Holy Communion, with Preparation, Thanksgiving, and other Prayers. 1d.; cloth, 2d.

LIVES OF ENGLISHMEN IN PAST DAYS. Four Series in 1 Vol. cloth gilt. 3s. 6d.
First Series, containing Herbert, Donne, Ken, Sanderson. 6d.
Second Series, Ketlewell, Hammond, Wilson, Mompesson, Bold, Jolly. 6d.
Third Series, Walton, Wotton, Fanshawe, Earl of Derby, Collingwood, Sadler, Exmouth. 10d.
Fourth Series, Alfred the Great, Sir T. More, John Evelyn. 1s.

LOCAL LEGENDS. By the author of "Cecil Dean." &c. 18mo., cloth 2s. 6d.
Contents:— The Legend of the Founder's Dream.—A Legend of S. Osmund's Priory.—The Barons' Tryst: A Legend of the "Roses."—The Lost Castilage, A Legend of Gatenhope Manor.—Furzy Fallow; or the Legend of Old Court.—Hove, A Legend of Sunshine.—Miss Mildred's Picnic; or the Legend of the Lake.

LORAINE.—Lays of Israel. By Amelia M. Loraine. 2s. 6d. cloth.

LOW.—The Translation of the Holy Scriptures, a Lecture delivered to the workmen of the London Lead Company, in the Company's School-room, Middleton in Teesdale. By John Low Low, M.A. Fcap. 8vo., 6d.

LUCY AND CHRISTIAN WAINWRIGHT, and other Tales. By the author of "The Wynnes," &c. Fcp. 8vo., 3s. 6d.

LYRA SANCTORUM; Lays for the Minor Festivals. Edited by the Rev. W. J. Deane. 3s. 6d.

MACAULAY.—A Day in Nismes. By S. E. Macaulay. 2s. 6d.

MACGREGOR, Cecilia.
Deepdene Mission; or, Shadows and Sunshine. Fcp. 8vo., 1s. 6d.
Summerford Priory. Crown 8vo., 4s. 6d.; cheap edition, 2s.

MAGNAY, The Rev. C.
Sermons, Practical and Suggestive. 4s.
Poems. New Edition, with Additions. 3s. 6d.

MAIDEN AUNT'S TALES, The. By the Author of "The Use of Sunshine," "Nina," &c. 3s. 6d.

MALAN, The Rev. S. C.
The Gospel according to S. John, translated from the Eleven Oldest Versions, except the Latin, and Compared with the English Bible, with Notes on every one of the Alterations proposed by the Five Clergymen in their Revised Version of this Gospel. Demy 4to. (Pub. 10s.) Reduced to 10s.
Meditations on our Lord's Passion. Translated from the Armenian of Matthew, Vardabed. 2s. 6d.
The Pocket Book of Daily Prayers, Translated from Eastern Originals. Suited for the Waistcoat Pocket. Cloth, 3d.; roan, 1s.
Prayers and Thanksgivings for the Holy Communion, chiefly for the use of the Clergy, Translated from Coptic, Armenian, and other Eastern Rituals. 1s. 6d.; calf, 3s.
Preparation for Holy Communion of the Body and Blood of Christ, with Prayers and Thanksgivings for the same; chiefly for the use of the Laity. Gathered and translated from Armenian and other Eastern Originals... 1s. 6d. cloth, 3s. calf,
Bethany, a Pilgrimage: and Magdala, a Day by the Sea of Galilee. 1s. 6d.
The Coasts of Tyre and Sidon. A Narrative. 1s.
Letters to a Young Missionary. 1s. 6d.
Plain Exposition of the Apostles' Creed, in Question and Answer. 1s. 6d.
Meditations for every Wednesday and Friday in Lent, on a Prayer of S. Ephraem. Translated from the Russian. 2s. 6d.
Companion for Lent. Being an Exhortation to Repentance, from the Syriac of S. Ephraem; and Thoughts for every Day in Lent, gathered from other Eastern Fathers and Divines. 1s. 3d.

MANUAL FOR COMMUNICANTS: being an Assistant to a Devout and Worthy Reception of the Lord's Supper. Roan, 1s.; paper cover, 6d. In large type, 6d.; also a cheap edition for placing in Prayer Books. 3d.

MANUAL FOR MOURNERS, with Devotions, Directions, and Forms of Self-Examination. Fcp. 8vo., 2s. 6d.

MANUAL of MORNING and EVENING PRAYER for a Christian Servant. 6d.

Manuals for Industrial Schools.
A cheaper re-issue, cloth, 6d. each; bound in One Vol., 2s. 6d.
No. I. Cooking; or, Practical Training for Servants, &c.
No. II. Gardening; or, Training for Boys as Gardeners.
No. III. Household Work; or, The Duties of Female Servants.
No. IV. Plain Needlework in all its branches.
No. V. On the Management of Poultry and Domestic Animals.

MARY MANSFIELD; or, the Life and Trials of a Country Girl. 6d.

MARK DENNIS; or, the Engine-Driver. A Tale of the Railway. By the Author of "The Clureter Brothers," &c. Second Edition. 18mo., 9d.

MASTERS'S LIST OF CHURCHES in which the Daily Prayers are said. New edition, with Map of the London Churches, 6d.

MAUNSELL.—Church Bells and Ringing. By the late W. T. Maunsell, M.A., Christ Church, Oxford. 1s.

MEDIEVAL ALPHABETS, Book of. Oblong 4to., 9s.

MEETING IN THE WILDERNESS, The; an Imagination. By the author of "The Divine Master." Wrapper, 1s.

MEMOIRS OF AN ARM-CHAIR, The. Written by himself. Edited by the author of "Margaret Stourton," "The Missing Sovereign," &c. 16mo., 1s.

MEMORIAL OF M.E.D. AND G.E.D. Brief notes of a Christian life and very holy death. By T.B.P. 6d.

MEMORIAL OF ELIZABETH A——. 6d.

MERCY DOWNER; or, Church and Chapel. 18mo., 6d.; cloth, 1s.

A METHOD OF ASSISTING THE SICK. Translated from the Latin. (A.P.F.) 8vo. rubricated, 9d.

MILL, The late Rev. W. H.
Sermons on the Nature of Christianity. 3s. 6d.
Sermons preached before the University of Cambridge, on the 5th of November and the following Sundays. 3s. 6d.

DR. MILL'S PORTRAIT. Proofs before letters, 10s. Proofs, 7s. 6d. Prints, 2s.

MILLARD.—S. Peter's Denials of Christ. Seven Short Lectures in the Boys of S. Michael's College, Tenbury. By the Rev. F. M. Millard, M.A. Fcap. 8vo., 2s., 1s. 2d.

MILLER.—Worshipping God in the Beauty of Holiness. By the Rev. R. Miller, M.A. 4d.

MILLIE'S JOURNAL; or, the Emigrant's Letters. Edited by the author of "Amy's Trials." Dedicated by permission to the Rev. H. Carwall, D.D. 6d.

MILMAN, The Right Rev. R., Bishop of Calcutta.
The Love of the Atonement; a Devotional Exposition of the 53rd chapter of Isaiah, 3rd edition, Fcap. 8vo. cloth, 2s. 6d.
Convalescence. Thoughts for those who are recovering from Sickness. Fcap. 8vo., 1s.
The Voices of Harvest. 4d., cloth, 1s.
The Way through the Desert; or, The Caravan. 5d.; 1s. cloth.
The Mystery of Marking; a Parable for School Girls. 4d., cloth 10d.
Meditations on Confirmation. 3d.

MINISTRATION OF PUBLIC BAPTISM OF INFANTS, to be used in Church, in combination with the Ministration of Reception to be used in the Church after the Private Baptism of Infants. 6d.

MINISTRY OF CONSOLATION, The. A Guide to Confession, for the use of Members of the Church in England. Second Edition. Limp cloth, 1s. 4d.

MINNIE'S BIRTHDAY, and other Tales for Children. By Marietta. Edited, and with Four Illustrations, by Cuthbert Bede. 2s., cloth.

MISERERE: the Fifty-first Psalm. With Devotional Notes. Reprinted from Neale's "Commentary on the Psalms." With additions by the Rev. S. F. Littledale, LL.D. 6d., cloth, 1s.

MITCHELL.—Hatherleigh Cross. A Tale. By Mrs. F. J. Mitchell. 16mo., cloth, 1s.

MONRO, The late Rev. E.
Sacred Allegories of Christian Life and Death. A Fine Edition, complete in one vol., printed on toned paper, and handsomely bound in cloth gilt. Crown 8vo., 7s. 6d.; morocco, 16s.

The Dark River.	The Ravellers, &c.
The Vast Army,	The Journey Home.
The Combatants.	The Dark Mountains.

Limp cloth, 1s. each. Cloth boards, 1s. 6d. each.
in 3 vols. cloth, 3s. 6d. each.

Basil, the Schoolboy; or, the Heir of Arundel. A Story of School Life. 4th edit. Fcap. 8vo., cloth, 2s. 6d.

Walter, the Schoolmaster; or, Studies of Character in a Boys' School. 3rd edit. Fcap. 8vo. cloth, 3s. 6d.

Tales for the Million. 18mo., complete, cloth, 2s.
Dick, the Haymaker, 4d.
Walter, the Convict, 4d.
Edward Morris. A Tale of Cottage Life. 2d.
The Tale of a Cotton Gown. Manchester Life. 4d.
Joey; or, the Story of an Old Coat, 5d.
Lella: A Tale in Verse, 1d.
Eustace; or, the Lost Inheritance. Fcp. 8vo., 2s.
Claudia, a Tale of the Second Century. 2s.; cheap edition, 1s.
The Footprints in the Snow. A Tale. 1s.
Leonard and Dennis; or, the Soldier's Life. A Tale of the Russian War. 4d.
Harry and Archie; or, First and Last Communion. Cloth, 1s.
Harry and Archie, with Sequel, in 1 Vol. cloth, 1s. 6d.
Nanny: a Sequel to "Harry and Archie." 6d.; cloth, 1s.
Parochial Papers. In limp cloth,
Readings and Reflections for Holy Week. 10d.
Plan of Preparation for Confirmation, for the use of the Clergy. 6d.
Manuals and Prayers for Confirmation and First Communion. Price 4d.
School Prayers for each day in the Week. 6d.
School Prayers for the Ecclesiastical Year. 1s.
The Schoolmaster's Day, with Hints for Lectures. 9d.
The above bound in one vol. cloth, price 4s.
True Stories of Cottagers. 18mo. cloth, or in a packet, 2s.
Midsummer Eve. 5d.; cloth 1s.
Pascal the Pilgrim. A Tale for young Communicants. 1s.; cloth, 1s. 6d.

C

MONSELL.—Prayers and Litanies, taken from Holy Scripture; together with a Calendar and table of Lessons. Arranged by the Rev. J. S. B. Monsell, LL.D. 18mo., cloth, 1s.

MOORE.—Easy Readings from the History of England. For the use of Little Children. By Mary E. C. Moore. Edited by the Rev. M. W. Mayow, M.A. 2nd edition, 18mo., 2s.

MORGAN, The Rev. A. M.
Gifts and Light. Church Verses. Fcap. 8vo. 3s.
The Ascension and other Poems. Fcap. 8vo. 6d.
The Church in Babylon and other Poems. Fcap. 8vo. 1s.

MORNING AND EVENING EXERCISES for Beginners. By a Clergyman. 3d., or 14s. per 100.

MORNING AND EVENING PRAYER. On a card. By E. S. 4d.

MORNING AND EVENING PRAYER, with Directions. By F. H. M. 2d.

MORNING AND EVENING PRAYERS for a Household. 4d.

MOSSMAN, The Rev. T. W.
A Glossary of the Principal Words used in a Figurative, Typical, or Mystical sense in the Holy Scriptures, with their Signification, gathered from the Sacred Writers themselves, or from the Works of the Ancient Fathers. Fcap. 8vo., cloth, 3s. 6d. Sermons. 12mo., cloth 3s.

MOULTRIE, The Rev. G.
Hymns and Lyrics, for the Seasons and Saints' Days of the Church. Fcap. 8vo., 6s. Family Prayer. A Lecture delivered before the Members of the Bristol Branch of the English Church Union, February 20, 1868. 6d.
Offices for Holy Week and Easter, after the Primer Use, together with the Meditations on the Life and Passion of our Lord. Edited by the Rev. G. Moultrie, M.A. 18mo. 3s.
The Martyrdom of S. Polycarp. 8vo., 1s.

MOUNTAIN, The late Rev. J. H. B.
Sermons for the Seasons, and on other occasions. Demy 8vo., cloth, 7s. 6d.
A Tract on Preparation for Death. By Desiderius Erasmus, of Rotterdam. Translated from the Latin by the Rev. J. H. B. Mountain, D.D. Fcap. 8vo., in large type. 2s.

MURRAY, Rev. F. H.
A Canon of Authorities with regard to the Altar and Eucharistic Sacrifice. 1s. 6d.
A Form of Self-Examination; with a Few Directions for Daily Use. 3d., or 21s. per 100.

MY DUTY AT THE TIME OF CONFIRMENT. On a thin card, 2s. 6d. per 100.

MY BIRTHDAY EVE. A Waking Dream. 1s. 6d.

NEALE, The late Rev. J. M.
History of the Holy Eastern Church.—General Introduction. Two vols., £1.
Appendix to the Introduction to the History of the Holy Eastern Church, containing a List of the Sees. 1s.
The History of the Patriarchate of Alexandria. Two vols., 24s.
Sermons preached in Sackville College Chapel. Four Vols., Crown 8vo.
Vol. I. Advent to Whitsun Day. With Introduction by the Editors. 7s. 6d.
Vol. II. Trinity and Saints' Days. 7s. 6d.
Vol. III. Lent and Passiontide. 7s. 6d.
Vol. IV. Sermons for the Black Letter Days, or Minor Festivals of the Church of England. Third Edition. 6s.
Sermons preached in a Religious House. 2 vols., fcap. 8vo., 10s.
Voices from the East. Documents on the Present State and Working of the Oriental Church. Translated from the Original Russ, Slavonic, and French, with Notes. 2s. 6d.
A Commentary on the Psalms, from the Primitive and Mediæval Writers; and from the various Office Books and Hymns of the Roman, Mozarabic, Ambrosian, Gallican, Greek, Coptic, Armenian, and Syriac Rites. By the Rev. J. M. Neale, D.D., and the Rev. R. F. Littledale, LL.D. Four Vols. Post 8vo. cloth, £2. 2s.
16s. 6d.
Vol. I. Third edition. Psalm I. to Psalm XXXVIII., with Three Dissertations.
Vol. 2. Second edition. Psalm XXXIX. to Psalm LXX. 10s. 6d.
Vol. 3. Psalm LXXXI. to Psalm CXVIII. 16s. 6d.
Vol. 4. Psalm CXIX. to CL. With Index of twelve thousand Scripture References. 16s. 6d.

NEALE, The late Rev. J. M.
  Ecclesiological Notes on the Isle of Man: a Summer Pilgrimage. 1s. 6d.
  Sequentiae Poems. Fcap. 8vo., 3s. 6d.
  Mediæval Hymns, Sequences, and other Poems, translated by the Rev. J. M. Neale. Second Edition. 2s.
  Hymns for the Sick: for the hours, days of the week, &c. 6d., cloth, 1s.
  Hymns for Children. First, Second, and Third Series. 2d. each. Complete in cloth, 1s.
  Songs and Ballads for Manufacturers. 3d.
  Stories of the Crusades. 2s.
  Duchenier, or the Revolt of La Vendée. 2s. 6d.
  The Unseen World; Communications with it, real or imaginary. New edition, with considerable additions. 3s. 6d.; cheap edition, 1s. 6d.
  The Followers of the Lord; Stories from Church History. 2s.
  Lent Legends. Stories for Children from Church History. 2s.
  Hierologus at Sackville College. 18mo., cloth 2s.
  The Egyptian Wanderers. A Tale of the Tenth Persecution. 18mo, 2s.
  Sunday Afternoons at an Orphanage. Sermons to Children. 2s.
  A Commentary on the Hymnal Noted, from Ancient Sources. 6d.
  Tales Illustrative of the Apostles' Creed. 2s. 6d.
  The Bible and the Bible only the Religion of Protestants. A Lecture. 4d.

NEDDIE'S CARE; or, "Suffer the Little Children." With eight Illustrations. 16mo., cloth, 1s. 6d.

NEVER TOO LATE TO MEND; or, the Two Fortune Tellers. By the author of "Willie Grant." 6d.

NEVINS. The Scriptural Doctrine of the Holy Communion. By the Rev. W. Nevins, 2s.

NEWLAND, The late Rev. H.
  Confirmation and First Communion. A Series of Sayings, Lectures, ..., ..., and Practical Catechism in relation to the preparation of Catechumens. Third edition. Fcap. 8vo., 7s. 6d.
  Tracts printed from the above for distribution. 1s packet, 1s. 4d.
  Three Lectures on Tractarianism, delivered in the Town Hall, Brighton, with Preface. New Edition. 1s.; cloth, 1s. 6d.
  Plain Short Sermons on the Parables, &c., adapted from the Fathers. Second Edition. Fcap. 8vo., cloth, 6s.
  A Memoir of the late Rev. Henry Newland, Vicar of St. Mary Church, Devon. By the Rev. K. M. .... With Portrait. 2s. 6d.

NORTHWODE PRIORY; A Tale, in Two Vols. By the Author of "Everley." 10s. 6d.

NOTICE OF .... Forms for filling up with Sponsors, &c. On a thin card, 11s. 8d. per 100.

NUGEE, The Rev. G.
  The Words from the Cross as applied to our own Deathbeds. A Series of Lent Lectures. Second Edition. Fcap. 8vo., 3s. 6d.

NUNN'S COURT; a Tale of Church Restoration. By Mrs. Frank Pettis. 18mo., cloth, 1s.

AN OFFERING TO S. MARGARET'S CONVENT. Dedicated with permission to the Mother Superior. Fcap. 8vo., cloth, 1s. 6d.

OGILVY.—The Nun of Brinklesterie. A Tale. In Six Songs. By Mrs. T. Ogilvy, (née Rosanquet,) author of "Hymns for Children of the Church of England," "Christian Lyrics," and "The History of our Blessed Lord in Verse." 8vo., 3s. 6d.

OLD COURT HOUSE, The. A Tale. 1s.

ONE STORY BY TWO AUTHORS; or, a Tale without a Moral. By J. L., Author of "A Rhyming Chronicle," and F. M. L., Author of "Gentle Influence," &c. Fcap. 8vo., 1s. 6d.

ORDER FOR MORNING AND EVENING PRAYER SIMPLY EXPLAINED. Edited by a Clergyman. 1s.
  By the same Author.
  The Litany Simply Explained. Fcap. 8vo., 6d.

ORDER FOR PRIME. Prayers for Early Morn. Price 1d.

ORDER FOR COMPLINE; or Prayers before Bed-time. 4d.

ORDER FOR SEXTS AND NONES. Prayers for 12 and 3 o'clock. 1d.

ORDINARY AND CANON OF THE MASS, according to the Use of the Church of Sarum. Translated, with Introduction and Notes, by John Theodore Dodd, B.A., late Junior Student of Christ Church, Oxford. 1s. 6d.

ORGANS (A short account of) built in England from the Reign of Charles the First to the present time. With designs by the late A. W. Pugin, Esq. Fcap. 8vo, 6s.

ORLEBAR.—Christmas Eve and other Poems. By Mrs. Cuthbert Orlebar. 1s.

OUR NEW LIFE IN CHRIST. Edited by a Parish Priest, C.L.C. Fourth edition. 18mo., cloth, 1s.; cheap edition, 6d.

A SEQUEL TO "OUR NEW LIFE IN CHRIST;" OR, THE PRESENCE OF JESUS ON THE ALTAR. With a Few Simple Ways of Worshipping Him at the Celebration of the Blessed Sacrament. To which are added, Devotions and Hymns. 18mo., limp cloth, 1s.; cloth boards, red edges, 1s. 6d.

OUR SOLAR SYSTEM: expanded from Notes of a Lecture delivered by a Country Curate. 6d.

AN OUTLINE OF THE CATHOLIC TRUTH. With Meditations thereon. 18mo., cloth, 2s.

OWEN.—An Introduction to the Study of Dogmatic Theology. By the Rev. Robert Owen, B.D. Demy 8vo., price 21s.

PAGET, The Rev. F. E.
　Sermons on the Saints' Days and Festivals. 3s. 6d.
　Sermons for Special Occasions. Containing twenty-one Sermons for Consecration of Churches, Churchyards, Restoration, Anniversary, Foundation Stones, New Schools, School Feast, Confirmation, Ordination, Visitation, Church and Educational Societies, Choirs, Wakes, Festivals, Clubs, and Assizes. Post 8vo. 5s.
　The Christian's Day. Royal 32mo., 2s. 6d., cloth.
　Surgam Corda: Aids to Private Devotion. Collected from the Writings of English Churchmen. Compiled by the Rev. F. E. Paget. A Companion to "The Christian's Day." 2s. 6d., cloth.
　Prayers for Labouring Lads. 1½d.
　Prayers for Young Women who have been taught in Church Schools. 1½d.
　Prayers on behalf of the Church and her Children in Times of Trouble. Compiled by the Rev. F. E. Paget. 1s.
　Trust upon Tombstones; or Suggestions for Persons intending to set up Monuments. With Engravings. 1s.
　Memoranda Parochialia, or the Parish Priest's Pocket Book. 3s. 6d., double size 5s.
　St. Antholin's; or, Old Churches and New. New edition. 4s.; cloth, 1s. 5d.
　The Owlet of Owlstone Edge: his Travels, his Experiences, and his Lucubrations. Fcap. 8vo., with a beautiful Steel Engraving. Fifth edition. 2s. 6d.
　The Curate of Cumberworth and the Vicar of Roost. 2s. 6d.
　The Warden of Berkingholt. 5s.
　Tales of the Village, a new edition, in one vol., 3s. 6d.
　How to Spend Sunday Well and Happily. On a card, 1d., or 7s. per 100.
　A Few Prayers and a Few Words about Prayer. 2d.
　How to be Useful and Happy. 2d.

PALMER.—Dissertations on some subjects relating to the "Orthodox" Communion. By the Rev. W. Palmer, M.A. 10s. 6d.

PARISH AND THE PRIEST, The. Colloquies on the Pastoral Care, and Parochial Institutions, of a Country Village. Reprinted from the "Churchman's" Companion." Fcp. 8vo., 2s. 6d.

PARISH TALES. Reprinted from the "Tales of a London Parish." In a packet, price 1s. 6d.

PARSONS.—Life-st-Eam Incumbents. Three Sketches. By Mark Parsons. 2s. 6d.

PASSION PLAY AT OBER-AMMERGAU. The English Words, by Mrs. Edward Childe. 1s.

PATH OF LIFE, The. By the author of the "Seven Corporal Works of Mercy." 6s.

PATHWAY OF FAITH, The, or a Manual of Instructions and Prayers. For the use of those who desire to serve God in the station of life in which He has placed them. Limp cloth, 1s.; cloth boards, 1s. 6d.

PATRICK, Bp.—The Parable of the Pilgrim. By Bishop Patrick. New Edition, 1s.

PEARSON.—Stories on the Eight Beatitudes. By the Rev. G. F. Pearson. 1s. cloth, or in a packet.

PEARSON.—Stories of Christian Joy and Sorrow, or Home Tales. By the Rev. H. D. Pearson, Containing Little Ruth Gray, Holy Stone, Herb, Old Oliver Dale. Price 1s.; separately, 4d. each.

PEOPLE'S HYMNAL, The, containing the Hymns, Carols, and Metrical Litanies. Wrapper, 6d.; limp cloth, 8d.; cloth boards, red edges, 1s.; roan, red edges, 1s. 9d. Large Type edition, cloth boards, 1s.; roan, 4s.

PEOPLE'S HYMNAL TUNE BOOK. Edited by Richard Redhead. Now publishing in Parts, 1s. each.

PERRY, The Rev. T. W.
Some Analogies between the Human and the Mystical Body, applied to Difficulties and Duties in the Church. Part I., Difficulties in the Church. 1s. 6d.
Some Historical Considerations relating to the Declaration on Kneeling, appended to the Communion Office of the English Book of Common Prayer: a Letter addressed privately in 1848, to the Right Rev. Charles H. Terrot, D.D., Bishop of Edinburgh and then Primus. Pp. 472, price 17s.
Directorium Sacramentum et Anglicanum. Directions for Celebrating the Holy Communion. Edited by the Rev. T. W. Perry. 18mo., 2s. 6d.
A Manual of Daily Prayers for Persons who are much hindered by the Duties of their calling. 4d.

PHILARET.—Select Sermons. Translated from the Russian. By Philaret, late Metropolitan of Moscow. With a Biography of the Author, and an Introduction by the Translator. Crown 8vo., cloth, 6s. 6d.

PHILLOTT.—Sacred Memories: The Athanasian Creed, metrically paraphrased, and other Poems. By the Rev. Francis Phillott, M.A., S. John's College, Oxford. Crown 8vo., m.; cloth, 3s. 6d.

PHIPPS.—Catechism on the Holy Scriptures. By the Rev. J. E. Phipps. 18mo. 1s.

PIOUS CHURCHMAN, The; a Manual of Devotion and Spiritual Instruction. 1s. 6d.; roan, 7s. 6d.

PLAIN WORDS ABOUT OUR LORD'S LIFE; or, How to Follow Christ. Parts I. and II., 6d. each; Parts III. and IV., 6d. each.

PLAIN WORDS TO CHORISTERS. 6d.

PLENDERLEATH.—The Parish Priest's Visiting List, with a Few Remarks on Parochial Visitation. By the Rev. W. C. Plenderleath, M.A. 1s. 6d.

POCKET MANUAL OF PRAYERS. Fourth edition, with considerable additions, 6d. Cloth, with the Collects, 1s.

POEMS. By C. A. M. W. Fcap. 8vo. 1s.

POLLOCK, The Rev. J. S.
Resting Places: A Manual of Christian Doctrine, Duty, and Devotion, for Private and Family use. 24mo., cloth, 1s. 6d.
The Plain Guide. 144 pp., 32mo., 4d.; cloth, 6d.
—— 32mo., wrapper, 4d.

POLLARD.—Avice; or, a Page from the History of Imperial Rome. By E. F. Pollard. Fcap. 8vo., 3s. 6d.

POOLE, The Rev. G. A.
Churches, their Structure, Arrangement, Ornaments, &c. 1s. 6d., cloth 2s. 6d.
History of England. From the First Invasion to Queen Victoria. New edition, Post 8vo., cloth, 7s. 6d.

POOR CHURCHMAN'S FRIEND, The. A Series of Tracts for the instruction of the Poor in Church Matters. 2d.

POPOFF, Basil.
    The History of the Council of Florence. Translated from the Russian by Basil Popoff. Edited by the Rev. J. M. Neale, D.D. 4s.
    The Origin and Composition of the Roman Catholic Liturgy, and its difference from that of the Orthodox Church. By Ivan Borovnitsky. Translated by Basil Popoff. Edited by the Rev. J. M. Neale, D.D. 8s.

POTT, The Ven. Archdeacon.
    Confirmation Lectures delivered to a Village Congregation in the Diocese of Oxford. 3rd edition, 8s.
    Village Lectures on the Sacraments and Occasional Services of the Church. Price 3s.

Practical Christian's Library.

Brechin's (Bishop of) Commentary on the Seven Penitential Psalms. 9d. and in cloth; 1s. 6d. bound.
The Art of Contentment. 1s. 6d.
Cosin's (Bp.) Collection of Private Devotions. 1s.; morocco, 3s. 6d.
Gerhard's Fourteen Meditations. 3d.
Ken's (Bishop) Practice of Divine Love. 9d.
Kettlewell's Companion for the Penitent. 3d.
The Young Churchman's Manual. Second Edition. 6d.
Nelson's Guide to the Holy Communion. 2d.
Patrick's (Bishop) Parable of the Pilgrim. 1s.
Sanderson's (Bishop) Christian Man a Contented Man. 9d.
Scudamore's Steps to the Altar. Cloth, 7s.
Snelling's Manual for Confirmation and First Communion. 5d.
Taylor's (Bishop) Life and Death of our Lord. 1s. 6d.
Taylor's (Bishop) Death, Judgment, Heaven, and Hell. 6d.

PRACTICAL SCIENCE OF THE CROSS IN THE USE OF THE SACRAMENTS OF PENANCE AND THE EUCHARIST. By M. the Abbé Gaos. Translated from the French. 18mo., cloth, 2s. 6d.; wrapper, 2s.

PRACTICE OF THE PRESENCE OF GOD THE BEST RULE OF A HOLY LIFE, being Conversations and Letters of Brother Lawrence. 2nd edition. Royal 32mo. sd.; cloth, 8d.

PRATT.—Letters on the Scandinavian Churches, their Doctrine, Worship, &c. By the Rev. J. B. Pratt, LL.D. Fcap. 8vo., 2s. 6d.

PRAYERS AND MAXIMS. In large type, 2s.; large paper, 3s. roan.

PRAYERS FOR CHOIRS IN THE VESTRY BEFORE AND AFTER SERVICE. Mounted, in folding roan case, 4s. 6d.

PRAYERS FOR THE SEVEN CANONICAL HOURS, together with Devotions, Acts of Contrition, Faith, Hope, and Love. 32mo. cloth, 1s.

Prayers.

Prayers for the Household for Morning and Evening. On a large Card, rubricated. 2d.
Prayers for a Husband and Wife. 2d. Ditto 6d.
Prayers for a Sick Room. 3s. 6d. per hundred.
Prayers for Different Hours of the Day. 3s. 6d. per hundred.
Prayers and Directions for Morning and Evening. By F.H. M. 8d.
Prayers for the use of Parochial Schools. By F. H. M. 4d.
Prayers for Working Men. By the Rev. W. J. Butler. 3d.
Daily Prayers for Labouring Lads. By the Rev. F. E. Paget. 1½d.
Daily Prayers for Young Women who have been taught in Church Schools. By the Rev. F. E. Paget. 1½d.
A Manual of Daily Prayers for Persons who are much hindered by the Duties of their calling. 4d.
The Hours of our Lord's Passion: being Short Prayers for the Sick, chiefly for the use of those engaged in nursing, either for themselves or their patients. 3d.
Short Prayers compiled for the Use of Penitants. 4d.
Meditations suitable for Lent and other Seasons of Penitence. Edited by the Rev. John Sharp, M.A. 3d.
Morning and Evening Prayers for a Family. 1½d., in wrapper 2d.
Short Morning and Evening Prayers for Working People. Card. 1d.
Short Devotions selected from the Book of Common Prayer. Chiefly for the use of Sick Persons. 2d.
Short and Simple Prayers for the use of Working Men with their Families. In fcap. 8vo. 4d.

PRAYERS FOR CHILDREN.
A Manual of Devotion for Schoolboys. Compiled by E. M. &d.
Simple Prayers for Little Children. By E. B. 2d., cloth, 4d.
Prayers for Young Persons. By A. H. 4d.; cloth, 6d.
Prayers for Little Children and Young Persons. 6d.; cloth, 8d.
Prayers and Directions to be held in daily Remembrance. In four parts. 1d.
Devotions for Children and Young Persons. 1d.
Prayers and Self-Examination for Children. 1d.
Simple Prayers for Morning and Evening for Working Boys. 1d.
Simple Prayers for Village Schools and Village Children. 1d.
Morning and Evening Prayers for Schools. ¼d.

A PRESBYTERIAN CLERGYMAN LOOKING FOR THE CHURCH. (Abridged.) 18mo., cloth, 2s.; cheap edition, 1s.

PRICHARD.—Sermons; by the late Rev. James Cowles Prichard, M.A. 4s. 6d.

PRIEST IN ABSOLUTION, The: a Manual for such as are called unto the Higher Ministries in the English Church. Part I. 2s. 6d.

PRIEST IN HIS INNER LIFE, The: Reprinted from "The Spirit of the Church." 1s.

PRIEST'S PRAYER BOOK, The, with a Brief PONTIFICAL. Containing Private Prayers and Intercessions, Offices, Readings, Prayers, Litanies, and Hymns, for the Visitation of the Sick; Offices for Bible and Confraternity Classes, Cottage Lectures, &c.; Notes on Confession and Direction; Remedies for Sin, &c., &c. Edited by two Clergymen. Fourth edition, much enlarged. Cloth, 6s.; limp calf, 9s.; limp morocco, 10s. With Common Prayer, 2s. 6d. additional.

Reprinted from "The Priest's Prayer Book."
Rehearsal to the Offices of the Sick, for the use of the Attendants. Cloth, 3s.
Parochial Offices, 1d.
School Offices. Third edition. 1d.
Office for a Regimental Synod, or Clerical Meeting. 1d.
Anglican Orders. A Summary of Historical Evidence. 1d.

PRIMER, (The) set forth at large with many Godly and Devout Prayers. Edited from the Post-Reformation Recension, by the Rev. Gerard Moultrie, M.A., Vicar of South Leigh. 4th Thousand. 16mo., cloth, 3s.
The Psalms, printed on toned paper and rubricated, 18mo., antique cloth, 3s.
The Hours of the Primer. Published separately for the use of individual members of a household in Family Prayer. 18mo., cloth, 1s.
Rubrics; see Litanies, Processions. Latin edition, 16mo., cloth, 1s.

PRISONERS OF CRAIGMACAIRE. A Story of "'45." Edited by the Author of "The Divine Master," &c. 1s.

PRYNNE, The Rev. G. R.
Plain Parochial Sermons. Second Series. Demy 8vo., 10s. 6d.
Eucharistic Manual, consisting of Instructions and Devotions for the Holy Sacrament of the Altar. From various sources. 1s. 6d., cloth; calf, 4s. 6d.; morocco, 5s. Cheap edition, limp cloth, 1s.; roan, 2s. 6d.
A Few Plain Words about what every Christian ought to Know, Believe, and Do in order to be saved. 2d.
Plain Instructions on Confirmation. 1d.
Plain Instructions on the Blessed Sacrament. Reprinted from the "Eucharistic Manual." 2d.

PSALTER, The: or Seven Ordinary Hours of Prayer, according to the use of the Church of Sarum. Beautifully printed and bound in antique parchment. Reduced to 18s.

PYE.—A Short Ecclesiastical History; from the conclusion of the Acts of the Apostles, to the Council of Nice, a.d. 325. By the Rev. H. J. Pye. 1s. 6d.

QUESTIONS AND ANSWERS ILLUSTRATIVE OF THE CHURCH CATECHISM. For the Use of Young Persons. New Edition. 6d. Cloth 6d.

QUESTIONS FOR SELF-EXAMINATION for the Use of the Clergy. 4d.

RAINE, Rosa.
Rose's Summer Wanderings. 5s.
The Queen's Isle. Chapters on the Isle of Wight, wherein Church Truths are blended with Island Beauties. Second edition. 2s. 6d.
Verses for Church Schools. 6d.

RAINY MORNINGS WITH AUNT MABEL; or, Incidents in Church Missions. 18mo., cloth, 2s. 6d.

READING LESSONS FROM SCRIPTURE HISTORY, for the Use of Schools. Royal 16mo., limp cloth, 6d.

READINGS FROM HOLY SCRIPTURE. By the author of "Tales of Kirkbeck." First Series, 1s. 6d. Second Series, 2s.

READINGS ON THE HISTORY OF JOSEPH AND HIS BRETHREN. Fcap. 8vo., 2s.; limp cloth, 2s.

RECOLLECTIONS OF A SOLDIER'S WIDOW. New Edition with Appendix. 6d.

REED.—Adventures of Olaf Tryggvesn, King of Norway. A Tale of the Tenth Century, showing how Christianity was introduced into Norway. By Mrs. J. J. Reed. 2s. 6d.

REFORMATION, Progress of the Church of England since the. 6d.; cloth, 9d.

REFORMED VILLAGE; or, Past and Present. Fcap. 8vo., 2d., 1s. 6d.; wrap. 1s.

REGISTER OF PERSONS CONFIRMED AND ADMITTED TO HOLY COMMUNION. For 600 names, 4s. 6d. For 1600 names 7s. 6d. half-bd.

REGISTER OF SERMONS, PREACHERS, AMOUNT OF OFFERTORY, &c. (As ordered by the 62nd Canon.) Fcap. 4to. bound, 4s. 6d.

REMINISCENCES OF FORTY YEARS. By an Hereditary High Churchman, 1s.

REVERENCE DUE TO HOLY PLACES AND HOLY THINGS. 6d.

RHYMES AND REASONS. Royal 8vo., 1s.
Contributions by the Revs. Professor Kennedy, D.D., W. Fraser, D.C.L., John Earle, M.A., C. Stanwell, M.A., R. Tomlins, M.A., S. J. G. Edwards, M.A., W. W. How, M.A., G. G. Woodhouse, M.A.; J. E. Hilary Skinner, Esq., Ellen J. Millington, Sarah A. Stanwall, Emilia Ellis, &c.

ROBERT AND ELLEN. 18mo., cloth, 1s.

ROBERTS, G. E.
Snowbound in Cleaberrie Grange. A Christmas Story. 2s. 6d.
Charley's Trip to the Black Mountain. 6d.

ROCHAT.—Harry's Help. By Mrs. S. C. Rochat. 1s.

ROCKSTRO, W. S.
Stories on the Commandments. The Second Table: "My duty towards my Neighbour." 1s. 6d. cloth, and in a packet.
Abbey Lands. A Tale. Fcap. 8vo. cloth, 5s.
The Choristers of S. Mary's. A Legend of Christmas-Tide. 4d.

ROOT OF THE MATTER, The; or the Village Class. 1s. 6d. cloth, 1s. wrapper.

RUSSELL.—Layer concerning the Early Church. By the Rev. J. F. Russell. 1s. 6d.

RUTH LEVISON; or, Working and Waiting. 1s. 6d.; paper cover, 1s.

SACRAMENTARIUM ECCLESIAE CATHOLICAE. A Sacramentary designed to incorporate the contents of all the Sacramentaries anywhere used in the Church, previous to the 13th century. Part I., Advent to Christmas. 2s. 6d. cloth; 1s. 6d. wrapper.

SAND, Louis.
Sylvester Enderby, the Poet. 2s. 6d.
Voices of Christmas. A Tale. 2s.

SANKEY.—Bible Exercises, adapted to the Services of the Church of England, and designed chiefly for Sunday Schools. By the Rev. Philip Sankey. Teacher's copy, and Pupil's copy, 6d.

SAVONAROLA, SCENES IN THE LIFE OF. By C. M. P. 18mo., cloth, 2s. 6d.

SCRIPTURE READING LESSONS FOR LITTLE CHILDREN. By a Lady. With a Preface by the late Bishop of Winchester. 1s. 6d. Second Series, 2s. Complete in one vol., 3s. 6d.

SCUDAMORE.—Increase for the Altar. A Series of Devotions for the Use of earnest Communicants, whether they receive frequently or at longer intervals. By the Rev. W. E. Scudamore,. Rector of Ditchingham. Royal 32mo., cloth, 2s. 6d.

SELECTIONS, NEW AND OLD. With a Preface by the late Bishop of Winchester. Fcap. 8vo. 4s. 6d.

SENTENCES from the Works of the Author of "Amy Herbert," selected by permission. 2s.

SERMONS REGISTER FOR TEN YEARS, by which an account may be kept of Sermons, the number, subject, and when preached. Post 4to., 1s.

SERVICE FOR CERTAIN HOLY DAYS, The. Being a Supplement to "The Day Hours of the Church of England." Crown 8vo., 2s.

SEVEN CORPORAL WORKS OF MERCY, illustrated in Seven Outline Engravings. 3s. 6d. plain; 5s. coloured. For hanging in Schools.

SEVEN SPIRITUAL WORKS OF MERCY, illustrated in Seven Outline Engravings. 3s. 6d. plain; 5s. coloured. For hanging in Schools.

SEVEN CORPORAL WORKS OF MERCY. In Verse. By the author of "The Daily Life of a Christian Child." With Illustrations. 6d.

SEVEN SPIRITUAL WORKS OF MERCY. In Verse. By the same author. Illustrated by Dalziel. 6d.

SEVEN PENITENTIAL AND FIFTEEN GRADUAL PSALMS, with the Litany and other Prayers and Collects. 32mo., 6d.

SHIPLEY, The Rev. Orby.
The Purgatory of Prisoners: or an Intermediate Stage between the Prison and the Public. 1s.
Eucharistic Meditations for a Month on the Most Holy Communion. Translated from the French of Avrillon. Limp cloth, 2s. 6d.
Daily Meditations: from Ancient Sources. Edited by the Rev. Orby Shipley. Advent to Easter. Cloth, 2s. 6d.
Daily Meditations for a Month, on some of the more moving truths of Christianity; in order to determine the Soul to be in earnest in the love and service of God. From ancient sources. Edited by the Rev. Orby Shipley. Cloth, 1s.
A Treatise of the Virtue of Humility, abridged from the Spanish of Rodriguez; for the use of persons living in the world. Cloth, 1s.
The Divine Liturgy: A Manual of Devotions for the Sacrament of the Altar. 1s.; cloth extra, 1s. 6d. Superior edition, toned paper, cloth boards, 2s. 6d.
The Daily Sacrifice: a Manual of Spiritual Communion. From Ancient Sources. Limp cloth, 1s.; cloth extra, 1s. 6d.
Considerations on Mysteries of the Faith, newly translated and abridged from the Original Spanish of Lois de Granada. 2s. cloth.
Avrillon on the Holy Spirit: Readings for Ascension and Whitsuntide. Translated and Abridged from the French of Avrillon. 1s.
Spiritual Exercises: Readings for a Retreat of Seven Days. Translated and abridged from the French of Bourdaloue. Edited by the Rev. Orby Shipley. 1s. 6d.
The Liturgies of 1549 and 1662 compared. Fcap. 8vo., cloth, 1s. 6d.

A SHORT OFFICE OF EVENING AND MORNING PRAYER for Families. 6d.

SHORT SERVICES FOR DAILY USE IN FAMILIES. Cloth, 1s.

SHORT DEVOTIONS FOR THE SEASONS; Compiled for Parochial Distribution, by F. H. M.
Devotions for the Season of Advent and Christmas. 1d., or 7s. per 100.
Devotions for Epiphany. 1d., or 7s. per 100.
Devotions for Lent. ½d., or 5s. 6d. per 100.
Devotions for Holy Week and Easter Eve. ½d., or 3s. 6d. per 100.
Devotions for Easter to Ascension. 1d., or 7s. per 100.
Devotions for the Festival of the Ascension. ½d., or 5s. 6d. per 100.
Devotions for Whitsuntide. ½d., or 3s. 6d. per 100.
Devotions for the Festival of the Holy Trinity. ½d., or 3s. 6d. per 100.
Devotions for Fridays. 1d., or 7s. per 100.
Complete in wrapper, 7d., cloth 9d.

SIMPLE WORDS ON THE LORD'S PRAYER. In large type. 6d.

SISTER ROSALIE, LIFE OF. By the author of "Tales of Kirkbeck." Second Edition. Cloth, 1s. ; cheap edition, 6d.

SISTERS OF CHARITY, and some Visits with them. Being Letters to a Friend in England. Two Engravings. 1s.

SKINNER, The Rev. J.
The Revelation of the Antichrist, and how to receive it. 1s. 6d.
Twenty-one Heads of Christian Duty, with Directions how to use them. 18mo., cloth, 1s.

SMITH.—Sermons preached in Holy Week. By the Rev. C. F. Smith, B.A. 6s.

SMITH.—The Church Catechism Illustrated by the Book of Common Prayer. By the Rev. Rowland Smith, M.A. 4d.

SMITH.—Grace Alford ; or, the Way of Unselfishness. By C. M. Smith. 18mo., 1s. 6d.

SMITH.—The Devout Chorister. Thoughts on his Vocation, and a Manual of Devotions for his use. By Thomas F. Smith, B.D. 32mo., cloth, 1s.
A Companion Book to the above, and may be had bound with it, in cloth, 1s. 6d.

EUCHARISTIC DEVOTIONS, with Preparations and Thanksgivings for Young Persons Unconfirmed or not Communicating. Royal 32mo., cloth, 9d.

SMYTTAN.—Cæsar Slighted and Rejected. Two Sermons, preached at S. Andrew's, Wells Street, in Passion and Holy Weeks, 1856. By the Rev. G. H. Smyttan, B.A. 1s.

SONNETS AND VERSES, from Home and Parochial Life. By the Rev. H. K. Cornish, M.A. 2s. 6d.

SPENCER.—Scenes of Suburban Life. By Anna B. F. Leigh Spencer. Fcap. 8vo. 4s. 6d.

SPERLING.—Church Walks in Middlesex ; being a Series of Ecclesiological Notes, with Appendix. By the Rev. John Hanson Sperling, M.A. 2s. 6d.

SPIRIT OF THE CHURCH, The. A Selection of Articles from the *Ecclesiastic*. Post 8vo. (Pub. 7s. 8d.) Reduced to 2s. 6d.

SPIRITUAL VOICES FROM THE MIDDLE AGES. Consisting of a Selection of Abstracts from the Writings of the Fathers, adapted for the Hour of Meditation, and concluding with a Biographical Notice of their Lives. 3s. 6d.

SPONSOR'S DUTY, The. To be given at Baptisms. 2s. 6d. per 100. On Card, printed in red and black. 14s.

STEERE.—An Historical Sketch of the English Brotherhoods which existed at the beginning of the 18th century. By Dr. Steere. 6d.

STEPS TO THE ALTAR : a Manual of Devotion for the Blessed Eucharist. By the Rev. W. E. Scudamore, M.A. 31st edition.

ROYAL 32mo., on toned paper, and rubricated.

	s.	d.		s.	d.
Cloth	2	3	Morocco or calf antique	7	6
French morocco	3	0	Ivory sides, gilt metal rims	10	6
Limp calf	4	6	Thick Ivory sides, best gilt		
Morocco	4	6	mountings	21	0
Kept also in a variety of gilt mountings, with clasps, crosses, &c.					

DEMY 18mo., (original edition.)

	s.	d.		s.	d.
Limp cloth	1	6	Limp calf	3	6
French morocco	2	6	Limp morocco	4	0

DEMY 18mo., in large type.

	s.	d.		s.	d.		s.	d.
Cloth boards	1	6	Limp calf	3	6	Limp morocco	4	0

IMPERIAL 32mo., cheap edition for distribution.

	s.	d.		s.	d.
Limp cloth	0	6	Roan, red edges	1	0

STONE, Mrs.
Eliza Morton, of the Pic-nic. 1s. 6d.
Handbook to the Christian Year, for Young People. 2s. 6d.

STORIES ON THE LORD'S PRAYER. By the author of "Amy Herbert." Price 6d.

STORIES FOR YOUNG SERVANTS. With Engravings. 18mo., cloth, 2s.

STORY OF A DREAM, or the Mother's Christian Version of Little Red Riding Hood. 1s.

STRETTON, The Rev. H.
Guide to the Todhra, Sick, and Dying. (Pub. 7s. 6d.) Reduced to 3s. 6d.
The Acts of S. Mary Magdalene Considered in Sixteen Sermons.
(Pub. 10s. 6d.) Reduced to 4s.
The Church Catechism explained and annotated principally as an aid to the Clergy in Catechising in Churches. Part I., 2s. cloth; Part II., the Creed, 4s.
The Church Catechism Explained, for the Aid of Young Persons. Part First. Abridged from the above. Price 2d.
The Child's Catechism. 1d.
A Catechism of First Truths of Christianity Introductory to the Church Catechism. ½d.
A Brief Catechism of the Bible. 6d.
The Scholar's Manual of Devotions, including the Church Catechism, &c. 3d.; cloth, 4d.

STRIDE.—Thirty Sketches for Christian Memorials, in sheet, 3s. 6d.

STUMPS. A Story for Children, with eight Illustrations. By Sophia Austin. 16mo., cloth, 2s. 6d.

SUCKLING, The late Rev. R. A.
Memoir, with Correspondence. By the late Rev. I. Williams, B.D. New Edition. Fcap. 8vo., 3s. 6d.
Sermons. Edited by the late Rev. I. Williams, B.D. New Edition. 3s. 6d.
Family Prayers adapted to the course of the Ecclesiastical Year. 6d.
Holiness in the Priest's Household. Second edition. 6d.
Manual for Confirmation and First Communion. Cloth, 6d.

SUMMERLEIGH MANOR; or, Brothers and Sisters. A Tale. Fcap. 8vo. 4s.

SUNDAY ALPHABET, The Little Christian's. 18mo., cloth, 1s.

SUNSETTING; or, Old Age in its Glory: a story of happiness, peace, and content. 18mo. 6d.

SUNTER'S DESIGNS FOR GRAVESTONES. On Sheets, 2s. 6d. each, by post 2s. 7d.
Nos. 1 and 2, Headstones; 3, Sepulchral Slabs; 4, Memorial Crosses.

SUSAN SPELLMAN. A Tale of the Silk Mills. By the Author of "Betty Cornwell." 6d.

SYDNEY, E. H. R.
A Chronicle of Day by Day. Fcap. 8vo., 5s.
A Life's Search. Fcap. 8vo., cloth 4s. 6d.
A Few Plain Words to Church-goers. 2d.

TALES FOR ME TO READ TO MYSELF. With 12 Engravings, 16mo., cloth, 2s. 6d.

TALES OF CROWBRIDGE WORKHOUSE. Blind Charlie; The Three Friends; Cousin Jane. By M. A. B. With a Preface by Louisa Twining. Fcap. 8vo., 2s., cloth, or the Tales separate in a packet.

TAYLOR, Bp. Jeremy, Prayers contained in the Life of Christ. Fcap. 8vo., cloth, 2s. 6d.

TEALE.—Lives of Eminent English Divines. By the Rev. W. H. Teale, M.A. With engravings, 5s.
Life of Bishop Andrewes, 1s.   Life of Dr. Hammond, 1s.
Life of Bishop Bull, 2d.   Life of Bishop Wilson, 1s.
Life of Judge of Nayland, 1s.

THINKING FOR ONESELF; or, an Adventure of the Catewes. Reprinted from "The Monthly Packet." By the late Editor of "Events of the Month," 18mo., 3s. cloth.

THOMPSON, The Rev. H.
Davidica. Twelve Practical Sermons on the Life and Character of David, King of Israel, published in 1827. Demy 8vo., 2s.
Concionalia; Outlines of Sermons for Parochial Use throughout the Year. New edition, 7s. 6d.
Concionalia. Second Series. 3s. 6d.
The Sunday School. A Lecture. Second edition, revised and enlarged. 4d.

THOUGHTS IN SOLITUDE. Post 8vo. 2s. 6d.

THREE HOURS AGONY: Meditations, Prayers, and Hymns on the Seven Words from the Cross of our Most Holy Redeemer, together with Additional Devotions on the Passion. Twelfth edition. 4d.

THRIFT; or, Hints for Cottage Housekeeping. By the author of " A Trap to Catch a Sunbeam." 1d.

TINY POLLIE'S UPS AND DOWNS. With Illustrations. By the author of " Neddie's Care." 16mo., cloth, 2s. 6d.

TOMLINE, The Rev. R.
Sermons for the Holy Seasons. 6s.
Tunbridge School Chapel. Stanzas. 1s. 6d., cloth.
Advent Sermons. First and Second Series in one vol. Second edition. 3s. 6d.
S. Mary's Home, Manchester. A Narrative of Facts. Stanzas, 1s.

TOMLINE, Bishop.—The Holy Scriptures, their Authenticity and Inspiration, Abridged from the " Elements of Christian Theology." 18mo. 1s. 3d.

TOWER BUILDERS; and THE TWO MERCHANTS: Two Allegories. 9d.

TROYTE.—Change-Ringing. An Introduction to the Early Stages of the Art of Church or Hand Bell Ringing, for the use of Beginners. By Charles A. W. Troyte, of Huntsham Court, Devonshire, a Member of the Ancient Society of College Youths, London. Second edition. Crown 8vo., cloth, 3s. 6d.; limp, 2s. The first six chapters separately in wrapper, 1s.

TRUST. By the Author of " The Beginnings of Evil." 18mo. 2s.

TWINS, The; or, "Thy Will be done." Price 6d.

TWO GUARDIANS, The; or, Home in this World. By the Author of " The Heir of Redclyffe." Fourth edition. 4s.

TWO FRIENDS, The; or Charley's Escape. By the Author of " Little Walter, the Lame Chorister," &c. 6d.

VALLEY OF LILIES, The. By Thomas à Kempis. 32mo., cloth, 6d., cloth gilt.

VANNY CROFT. By the Author of " Contrasted Christmas," &c. 18mo., cloth, 2s.

VERSES FOR CHRISTIAN CHILDREN ON THE DUTIES, TRIALS, AND TEMPTATIONS OF THEIR DAILY LIVES. By the author of " The Daily Life of the Christian Child." Edited by the Rev. J. R. B. Monsell, LL.D., Rector of S. Nicholas', Guildford. 6d.; cloth, 9d.

VERSES FOR THE SUNDAYS AND HOLIDAYS OF THE CHRISTIAN YEAR. By the Author of the " Daily Life of the Christian Child," &c., with Illustrations. 1s.

VICTORIA AND HER CONTEMPORARY SOVEREIGNS. 18mo., 6d.

VIDAL, Mrs. F.
Home Trials. 18mo., cloth, 2s.
Esther Merle, and other Tales. 1s. 6d.

A VILLAGE STORY FOR VILLAGE MAIDENS. In Three Parts. Susan, Esther, and Dorothy; or, the Three Starts in Life. 18mo., cloth 2s. 6d.

A VOYAGE TO THE FORTUNATE ISLES. An Allegory of Life. 1s., cloth 1s. 6d.

WALCOTT, The Rev. M. E. C.
The Interior of a Gothic Minster. A Lecture delivered at the Architectural Museum, South Kensington, April 28, 1864. Demy 8vo., 1s.
The Precinct of a Gothic Minster. A Lecture delivered before the Cambridge Architectural Society, 1864, and the Architectural Museum, 1865. 1s.
Cathedralia. A Constitutional History of Cathedrals of the Western Church. 8vo., 8s.

WARING.—Annuals and Perennials; or, Seed-time and Harvest. By C. M. Waring. Demy 8vo., beautifully illustrated, 8s.

WAS IT A DREAM? and THE NEW CHURCHYARD. By the Author of " Amy Herbert." 1s. 6d.; paper, 1s.

WATSON, The late Rev. A.
The Seven Sayings on the Cross. Sermons. 1s. 6d.
Jesus the Giver and Fulfiller of the New Law. Eight Sermons on the Beatitudes. 3s. 6d.
Sermons for Sundays, Festivals, Fasts, &c. Edited by the late Rev. A. Watson, M.A. 2s. 6d. each.
2nd Series, 2 vols.—1st Sunday in Advent to the 25th Sunday after Trinity.
3rd Series, 1 vol.—Some occasional offices of the Prayer Book.
A Catechism on the Book of Common Prayer. 2s.

WEST, The Rev. J. H.
A Short Treatise on the Holy Eucharist. Fcap. 8vo., 2s. 6d.
Parish Sermons on the Chief Articles of the Christian Faith. 6s.
Parish Sermons on the Ascension of our Lord. Fcap. 8vo., 3s. 6d.
On the Figures and Types of the Old Testament. 1s. 6d.
The Memorial before God. Crown 8vo., 3d.
Questions and Answers on the Chief Truths of the Christian Religion, for the assistance of younger Teachers and Monitors. 1d. or 7s. per 100.
Questions on the Chief Truths of the Christian Religion, intended for the use of higher classes. 3d.
" What mean ye by this Service?" Exodus xii. 16. Some Account of the Meaning of the Chief Service of the Christian Religion. 4d.
Reasons for being a Churchman. Founded on the Holy Scriptures. Cheap edition, for distribution, 1½d.
Tracts on Church Principles. Nos. 1 to 12, cloth, 1s. 6d.
Prayers and Hymns for Sunday Schools. 2d.
A Catechism on the Church. New edition, 4d.
A Catechism on the Two Principal Types of Holy Baptism, with Questions upon our Name. Fifth edition, 2d.
A Catechism on the Chief Truths concerning our Lord and Saviour Jesus Christ. Intended chiefly for the use of Sunday Schools. A revised edition. 2d.

WHYTEHEAD.—College Life. Letters to an Undergraduate. By the late Rev. T. Whytehead. New edit. Edited by the Rev. W. N. Griffin, M.A. 2s. 6d.

WILFORD, Florence.
Play and Earnest. A Tale. Fcap. 8vo. cloth, 5s.
The Master of Churchill Abbots, and his Little Friends. 4s. 6d.
A Maiden of Our Own Day. Fcap. 8vo., 6s.
An Author's Children. 18mo., 1s.
The King of a Day; or Glimpses of French Life in the Fifteenth Century. 18mo., 2s.

WILBRAHAM, Frances M.
The Loyal Brait, and other Tales for Boys. Translated from the German. With Engravings. 2nd Edition. 2s. 6d. cloth; 1s packet, 2s.
History of the Kingdom of Judah, from the Death of Solomon to the Babylonish Captivity. 18mo., cloth, 1s. 6d.

WILKINS.—Threescore Years and Ten. By the late G. Wilkins, D.D., Archdeacon of Nottingham. 2s. 6d.

WILKINS.—Early Church History. A Lecture delivered before the Literary Society, Southwell, Notts, December 12, 1854. By the Rev. F. M. Wilkins. 6d.

WILKINSON, The Rev. J. B.
Mission Sermons. Twenty-five Plain Sermons preached in London and Country Churches and Missions. By John Bourdieu Wilkinson, B.A., Senior Assistant Priest of S. Paul's, Knightsbridge. Fcap. 8vo., Second edition, 3s. 6d.
Mission Sermons. Second Series. Fcap. 8vo. cloth. 3s.
The Hour of Death. A Manual of Prayers and Meditations intended chiefly for those in sorrow or in sickness. Royal 32mo., 2s.

WILLIAMS, The late Rev. I.
The Altar, or Meditations in Verse on the Holy Communion. By the author of "The Cathedral." 3s. 6d.
Hymns on the Catechism. 3d., cloth 1s.

WINDSOR.—Sermons for Soldiers. Preached at Home and Abroad. By C. D. Windsor, M.A., Chaplain to the Forces. Fcap. 8vo., 3s. 6d.

WINGED WORDS. By A. H. 2s. 6d.

A WINTER IN THE EAST, in Letters to the Children at Home. By F. M. 18mo., 3s.

WOODFORD, The Right Rev. J. R., D.D., Bishop of Ely.
Sermons preached in various Churches of Bristol. 2nd Edition, 7s. 6d.
Occasional Sermons. Vol. I., 7s. 6d, Vol. II., 7s. 6d.
Ordination Sermons preached to the Dioceses of Oxford and Winchester, 1869—1878.
8vo., 8s. 6d.

WOODHOUSE.—The Exemplar of Penitence. Meditations on Psalm 51, for the
Sundays in Lent, and other Times. By the Rev. F. C. Woodhouse, M.A., Rector of
S. Mary's, Hulme. 18mo., 1s. 6d.

WOODWARD.—Demoniacal Possession; its Nature and Cessation. A prize essay.
By the Rev. T. Woodward, M.A. 2s.

WROTH.—Five Sermons on some of the Old Testament Types of Holy Baptism. By
the Rev. W. R. Wroth, B.A. Post 8vo., cl., 2s.

WYNNES, The; or, Many Men, Many Minds. A Tale of every-day life. Fcap. 8vo.,
cloth, 3s.

YORKE.—Cottage Homes; or, Tales on the Ten Commandments. By Miss H. Yorke.
18mo., cl., 2s.; or the Tales separately, in a packet, 2s.

YOUNG CHURCHMAN'S ALPHABET. By the Author of "The Grand-
father's Christmas Tale," &c. With Illustrations of the chief events in our Lord's
Life, drawn and engraved by R. and H. Dudley. 6d.

CHURCH MUSIC.

BY RICHARD REDHEAD.

Book of Tunes adapted to "Hymns Ancient and Modern."

One Hundred and Ninety-seven Hymn Tunes for the several Seasons of
the Christian Year. With an Appendix, and Index of Tunes to "Hymns Ancient and
Modern." Demy 8vo., cloth, 4s ; Vocal Score, 2s.

A Set of Ten Tunes for Advent, Epiphany, Lent, Easter, Ascension,
Whitsuntide, Fridays, and All Saints, arranged from Dr. Tye (1553).
Words interlined, 2s. 6d.

The Music of the Introits. Containing Introits for all the Seasons from Advent
to Advent, with the occasional Festivals. 6s.

Responses to the Commandments, Creeds, Offertory Sentences, Sanctuses, and Glorias. 8s.

Music for the Office of the Holy Communion, (Second Series) containing
four Kyries; two Sanctuses; the Lord's Prayer (after the Communion) harmonized,
founded on Merbecke; four Glorias in Excelsis. 3s. 6d.

The Offertory Sentences from the Book of Common Prayer. The Music
arranged from Merbecke. 3s. 6d.

Two Offertory Anthems. 1s.

The Anthems for the Seven Days before Christmas, and for Good
Friday. 3s. 6d.

"O My People, what have I done unto thee?" Anthem for Good Friday. 1s.

Hymns and Canticles used at Morning and Evening Prayer. Pointed and
set to the Ancient Psalm Tones. 2s. 6d.

"Who are these like stars appearing?" Hymn for All Saints' Day. 1s.

Miserere mei, Deus. Psalm 51, as sung in the Communication Service. 7d.

The Order for the Burial of the Dead. Printed from the Book of Common
Prayer; the Musical Notation (from Merbecke's Books of Common Prayer Noted,
1550) Harmonized. Intended for the use of Choirs. 6d.

Music for the Offices of the Holy Eucharist: being the Kyrie Eleison, Credo,
Sanctus, Benedictus, Agnus Dei, and Gloria in Excelsis, set to music for the especial
use of Parish Choirs. Imperial 8vo., 1s.

BY THE REV. T. HELMORE, M.A.

S. Mark's Chant Book. (In daily use at S. Mark's College Chapel, Chelsea.) 4s. 6d.
Part I. The Chants in full for each Morning and Evening. 2s. 6d.
Part II. The Table of the Chants. 1s.

Hymnal Noted, or Translations of the Ancient Hymns of the Church, set to their proper melodies. Cloth, 5s.

Accompanying Harmonies to the Hymnal Noted. Royal 8vo., 10s. 6d.

Accompanying Harmonies to the Psalter Noted. 8s.

Accompanying Harmonies to the Brief Directory of Plain Song. 1s. 6d.

Manual of Plain Song. The Canticles and Psalter together. 3s. 6d. cloth; royal 8vo., cloth, 5s.

BY H. J. GAUNTLETT, MUS. DOC.

The Psalter, or Psalms of David, pointed as they are to be sung in Churches, adapted to the Ancient Church Tones. Cloth, 1s.

The Canticles of Morning and Evening Prayer, with the Creed of S. Athanasius, adapted to the Church Tones. 4d.

Choral Services of the Book of Common Prayer, as appointed to be sung.
Part I. The Canticles, Versicles, and Responses for Morning and Evening Prayer. Part II. The Athanasian Creed, the Litany, and Office of Holy Communion. In full score, suited to Cathedrals, Parish Choirs, &c. Royal 8vo., bold music type, price 1s. 6d. each Part, or bound together in cloth, price 3s. 6d.

The Canticles in the Morning and Evening Services, pointed correctly for chanting, with chants varied to suit the character of the words. 4d., cloth 6d.

BY THE REV. T. F. RAVENSHAW, M.A., AND W. S. ROOKSTRO, ESQ.

The Ferial Psalter; together with the Canticles adapted to Ancient Ecclesiastical Tones. Fcap. 8vo., cloth, 2s. 6d.
The Psalter separately, limp cloth 1s. 6d.

The Canticles adapted to Ancient Ecclesiastical Tones. Fcap. 8vo., 9d.

Accompanying Harmonies to the Ferial Psalter, with Harmonies for Additional Chants and the Ambrosian Te Deum. By W. S. Rookstro, Esq. imp. 8vo., 4s.

BY FREDERICK HELMORE, ESQ.

A very Easy Burial Service, for Village Choirs. 8vo., 6d.

Te Deum Laudamus, Nos. 1, 2, 4, set to Short Chants. 2d. each.

Te Deum Laudamus, No. 3, Benedicite, and the Athanasian Creed, set to Short Chants. 3d.

Te Deum Laudamus, Nos. 1 to 4, set to Short Chants, in one book. 6d.

The Canticles, set to Short Chants. 3d.

Te Deum Laudamus, set to Short Chants with varied Harmonies. By the Rev. J. Schoralty. 3d.

The Canticles arranged for Antiphonal Chanting according to the Anglican Use. By the Rev. R. F. Lawrence, M.A., Vicar of Cubgrove, Oxon. The Verses printed alternately in red and black. In Two Parts. Price 1s.

Ancient English Choral Services of the Sixteenth Century. Edited by the Rev. John Jebb, D.D. 1s.
I. Venite exultemus. II. Communion Service by Thomas Causton.

Burial Office Noted, for Parochial Use. 6d.

Hymns of the Church. Pointed as they are to be Chanted; together with the Versicles, Litany, Responses, &c., by T. Tallis. Arranged by Mr. Fearnall. 1s.

Kyrie Eleison; or, Responses to the Commandments. Compiled from a Quintett by Winter. 4d.

The Prefaces in the Office of the Holy Communion, with their Ancient Chant. By the Rev. J. L. Crompton. M.A. Pr. 6d.

Music as sung in the Church of S. Paul, Newton Abbot, Devon. Compiled from Merbecke and other Authentic Sources, and arranged in a simple form for Ordinary Days. By George O. Browne, Organist. Kyrie Eleison, 2d.; Preces and Responses, 4d.

Te Deum, Jubilate, Sanctus, Kyrie, Magnificat, and Nunc Dimittis. Four Parts and Accompaniment. By T. L. Fowle, Mus. Doc. 2s. 6d.

Ninety-five Chants, Ancient and Modern, appropriated to the Canticles. By the Rev. C. S. Groeber, B.A. Feap. 4to., 1s.

Te Deum, set to a simple chant for Village Choirs. By the Rev. J. W. Rumsey. 1d.

Gregorian and other Chants, adapted to the Psalter and Canticles, as pointed to be sung in Churches. 1s. 6d.

The Eight Gregorian Tones, with their several endings separately. 1d.

Dies Irae. Translated into English metre, by W. J. Irons, D.D., with the Music, by Charles Child Spencer, Esq. 3s. 6d. English Words, 3s. 6d. per 100.

Dies Irae. Set to easy Music in short score by the Rev. H. F. Havergal. 3d. Suited to Parish Choirs and Schools.

Hymns of the Holy Eastern Church. Set to Music for Four Voices, by E. Sedding. Fcap. 4to. 1s.

S. Michael's Hymns. Containing "O Paradise;" "The Land beyond the Sea;" "Holy Spirit, Lord of Light." The Music composed by Edwin Linter. Third edition. 6d.

Hymns of the Eastern Church, The Endless Alleluia, and other Hymns. Set to Music and Dedicated to the Right Rev. the Lord Bishop of Rochester, by Arthur Henry Brown, Organist of Brentwood, Essex. 4to., 1s.

"Jerusalem the Golden," from the Rhythm of Bernard de Morlaix, set to Music in Four Parts, by Edmund Sedding. 2d.

"Sun of my Soul." From the "Christian Year." Set to Music in Four Parts, by Edmund Sedding. 1d.

Hymn for the Opening of a New School. 1d.

Confirmation Hymn. 1d.

"Art thou Weary, art thou Languid?" Four Part Hymn. Composed by Robert Parker. The Words from Dr. Neale's "Hymns of the Eastern Church." 0d.

CAROLS.

Christmas Carols. In sets of Four, 6d. each set; or bound together, 1s. 6d. The Words alone, 1d.

"Last Night I Lay a Sleeping." A Christmas Carol. The Music by N. J. Gauntlett, Mus. Doc. 6d.

"Hark to the Merry Bells." A Christmas Carol in Duet, Chorus, and Solo. The Words and Music composed by T. L. Fowle, Mus. Doc. 1s.

The Poor Man's Christmas Carol. On Card, with Music, 1d.

Divers Carols for Christmas and Sundry Tydes of Holy Church, with apt Notes to sing 'em withall, newly set forth in fit and sober Composure. By Arthur Henry Brown. 1s. 6d.

"When Christ was Born." A Christmas Carol, from the Harleian MS. in the British Museum. Set to Music by A. H. Brown. Dedicated to the Bishop of Oxford. 1s.

A Carol for New Year's Day. Set to Music by A. H. Brown. Dedicated to the Bishop of Brechin. 1s.

An Epiphany Carol. Set to Music by A. H. Brown. Dedicated to the Rev. Dr. Pusey. 1s.

Easter Carol. Set to Music by A. H. Brown. Dedicated to the Bishop of Salisbury. 1s. 6d.

"Joyful Rise, O Christian People!" Music by the Rev. G. H. Curtis. Words by the Rev. A. H. Wyatt. "Wake, Christian Children!" Words and Melody by the Rev. S. C. Hamerton. 4d.

"Joy and Gladness." A Christmas Carol. Written to an Ancient Melody, by the Rev. J. M. Neale, M.A. Harmonized for Four Voices, with or without accompaniment, by the Rev. S. S. Greatheed, M.A. 6d.

A Collection of Ancient Carols for Christmas and other Tides. Arranged for Four Voices. By Edmund Sedding, Editor of "Ancient Christmas Carols," &c. 1s. 6d. Words 1½d.

Dives and Lazarus. A Christmas Carol, written to an old melody by the late Dr. Neale, not hitherto published, and arranged for four voices. By Edmund Sedding. 2d.

"Tell again the olden Story." A Christmas Carol, for Four Voices. On toned paper, 1½d.

An Easter Carol. The melody of a Sequence of the Thirteenth Century, with Accompaniment; the words from two ancient Carols. By the Rev. J. M. Neale. 3d;

"We have Risen very Early." Carol for Mayday. The Words from the "Old Church Porch." Composed and arranged for Four Voices, by the Right Rev. H. L. Jenner, late Bishop of Dunedin. 2d.

Hymns for Little Children. By Mrs. C. F. Alexander. Set to Music by Dr. Gauntlett. Suitable for Schools or Families. 1s. 6d.; cloth 4s.

Hymns for Little Children. Set to Music by E. C. A. Cheyuell. Parts I. and II. 1s. each.

Morning and Evening Hymns. From the "Hymns for Little Children," set to Music for the use of Schools and Families. By Dr. Gauntlett. 3d. each.

Narrative Hymns for Village Schools. By Mrs. C. F. Alexander. Set to Music for one or two voices by A. F. 2s. 6d.

Accompanying Tunes to the Hymns for Infant Children. Edited by the Rev. J. B. Dykes, M.A., Mus. Doc. 1s.

The Child's Grace before and after Meal. Set to simple music, by Dr. Gauntlett. 2d.

Prose Hymn for Children. By the Rev. W. J. Jenkins, Rector of Fillingham. 7s. per 100.

"He is coming, He is coming." Hymn for Advent. Words by Mrs. C. F. Alexander. Music by the Rev. E. Y. Cadd, M.A. 3d., on card 6d.

Harvest Hymn, "O sing the Song of Harvest." By R. C., from the *Guardian*. Set to Music for Four Voices, suitable for ordinary Choirs. By the Rev. Henry E. Havergal, M.A. 4d.

Harvest Hymn. Words by the Rev. J. M. Neale. The Music composed by Henry G. Duffield. 6d.

King Alfred's Hymn. "As the Sea to brighter Skies." Arranged to ancient music, by Dr. Smith. 2d.

"The Threefold Heavens of Glorious Height." The words from the "Cathedral." The Music by M. A. W. 1s.

A Song for the Times. Words by the Rev. J. M. Neale. The Music (arranged for Four Voices) by the Rev. J. W. Rodway. 3d.

"The Better Land." The Poetry by Mrs. Hemans. The Music by R. Redhead. Dedicated to the Rev. W. U. Richards. 3s.

Collects for the Fourth and Seventeenth Sundays after Trinity. The Music by Mrs. William Warren. Dedicated to the Most Honourable the Marchioness of Lansdowne. 1s.

The Chorister's Hymn. On Card, 4d.

Eighty Short Exercises in Eight Lessons on the Major Scale. By F. Helmore. 4d.

PAMPHLETS.

Anglican Orders. A Summary of Historical Evidence. Reprinted from "The Priest's Prayer Book." 1d.

Austen's (Rev. S. C.) Prayers for the Dead a Universal Practice in the Church. 4d.

Baxter's late Rev. W. R.) The Gainsaying of Core in the Nineteenth Century. Addressed to all who call upon the Name of Jesus Christ our Lord. Second edition. 6d.

Barker's (Rev. W.) Use and Abuse of Church Bells. 6d.

Blunt's (Rev. J. H.) Three Essays on the Leading Principles of the Reformation, illustrating its Catholic Character from its Constitutional, Doctrinal, and Ritual History. 4d.

Burges' (W.) Iconography of the Chapter House, Salisbury. 1s.

Chambers' (Rev. J. C.) The English Reformation: when made, when marred, when mended. 2d.

Chamberlain's (Rev. T.) The Chancel, an Appeal for its proper use, addressed to Architects, Church Restorers, &c. 6d.

Church (The) and Public Opinion. 2d.

Dawson's (Rev. W.) The Supremacy of S. Peter not to be found in Holy Scripture. 3d.

Duty and Blessedness of Intercessory Prayer. 2d.

Ecclesiological Society's Publications.

A Few Words to Churchwardens on Churches and Church Ornaments. No. II. Suited to Town or Manufacturing Parishes. 3d.

A Few Words to Church Builders. Third edition, entirely rewritten. 1s.

A Few Words to Parish Clerks and Sextons. Designed for Country Parishes. 1d.

Advice to Workmen employed in Building a Church. On a Sheet for distribution or suspension in Vestry Rooms. 1d.

On the History of Christian Altars. A Paper read before the Cambridge Camden Society. Second edit. 6d.

Church Schemes; or, Forms for the classified description of a Church. Sixteenth edition, in folio and 4to., 1s. per dozen.

Twenty-four Reasons for getting rid of Church Pews. Ninth edit. 1d., or 3s. per 100.

The Church of the Holy Sepulchre, Cambridge. Some Account of the Church and its restoration, with an audited Statement of the Treasurer's Account. 6d.

Funerals and Funeral Arrangements. 1s.

Fowle's (Rev. H.) The Epistle to the Hebrews, the Epistle of S. Paul. 3s. 6d.

Goodwin's (Dean) Suggestions for a Code of Canons for a Province deriving its origin from the Church of England. 2s.

Gresley's (Rev. W.) Idealism Considered, chiefly with reference to a Volume of "Essays and Reviews" lately published. 1s.

Grueber (Rev. C. S.)
Holy Baptism: a complete Statement of the Church's Doctrine. 1s. 6d.
Plain Discourse on the One Faith. 1s.
Letter on the Proposed Alteration of the Order for the Burial of the Dead, 1s.

Hammond's (Rev. J.) The Law and Usage of the Church of England on certain disputed points of Ritualism. 6d.

Hogarth (Rev. W.)
The Doctrine of the Church on the Divinity of our Lord Jesus Christ. 1s.
Rationalism in the Church of England. An Essay, in Six Parts, (reprinted from the Ecclesiastic,) revised and enlarged, with an appendix on "Essays and Reviews." 8vo., 1s. 6d.
Passive Theology. An Essay, reprinted (with additions) from the Ecclesiastic. 8vo., 1s. 6d.

Hubbard's (J. G.) The Attendance of Non-Communicants at the Administration of Holy Communion. 3d.

Littledale (Rev. R. F.)
On the Application of Colour to the Decoration of Churches. 6d.
Religious Communities of Women in the Early and Medieval Church. 1s.

Miller (Rev. Charles.)
Plea for the Revival of the Study of the Common Law, in a Letter to the Earl of Derby. 3d.
Plea for Moral Philosophy and Law, in a Second Letter to the Earl of Derby. 6d.

MELLAKE'S (Rev. E. J., B.D.) A Practical Guide to the Services of the Church of England. 3d.

MONRO'S (Rev. E.) The Church and the Million. Five Letters. 1s.

Our Difficulties and the Way to deal with them. By a Working Clergyman. 6d.

PINDER'S (Rev. H. S.) Plea for Country Bishops. 6d.

Position of the Priest at the Altar. 6d.

PROCTOR'S (Rev. C. M.) The History of the Church in the First Seven Chapters of the Acts, with Remarks Doctrinal and Practical suited to these times. 6d.

RAINE'S (Rev.) The Restoration of the Jews, and the Duties of English Churchmen in that respect. 1s.

RUSSELL'S (Rev. J. F.) Anglican Ordination Valid. A Refutation of certain Statements in "The Validity of Anglican Ordinations Examined, by the Very Reverend Peter Richard Kenrick, V.G." 1s.

Right of all the Baptized to be present at the Celebration of the Holy Eucharist. 6d.

Sunday Schools; their Use and Abuse. By a Teacher of some Years' Experience. Reprinted with additions from "The Churchman's Companion." Fcap. 8vo. 1d.

STRONG'S (Bishop of) Letter on Collections at the Offertory. 4d.

Thoughts on Religious Communities, being the Letters of Two Friends. 3d.

Two Ways of Christian Life. 6d.

TODD (Rev. T.)
The Creeds, Articles, and Homilies, their Origin, Authority, and Interpretation. 1s.
The Bible without the Church, a Letter to Lord Shaftesbury. 6d.

WALCOTT (Rev. M. E. C.)
The Interior of a Gothic Minster. 1s.
The Precinct of a Gothic Minster. 1s.

What have Thirty Years of Church Revival done? 3d.

WEST (Rev. J. R.)
A Distinctive Vestment for the Celebration of the Holy Eucharist required by Common Sense, sanctioned by Holy Scripture, used by the whole Catholic Church, and ordered by the Rubrics of the Church of England. 6d.
The North End Unhistorical, Unrubrical, Unmeaning, and Irreverent towards Almighty God. 6d.

Women and their Work. 6d.

WRAY'S (Rev. C. D.) Inquiry respecting the Vestments of the Anglican Church. 3d.

SINGLE SERMONS.

ANDREWES' (Bishop) The Duty of a Nation in time of War. A Sermon preached before Queen Elizabeth. 6d.

BAILEY'S (Rev. W.) The Law of Divine Growth. Preached at S. Mary's, Plaistow, on the Octave of its Re-opening. 3d.

BARTHOLOMEW'S (Ven. Archdeacon) The Holiness of Baptised Infants. Preached at Morchard Bishop. 6d.

BENNETT'S (Rev. W. J. E.) "Christ Jesus came into the World to save Sinners." A Sermon preached in the Parish Church of S. George in the East. 6d.

BODY'S (Rev. G.) The Present State of the Faithful Departed. A Sermon preached in substance at All Saints' Church, Margaret Street, on Sunday, June 22, 1873, being the Sunday after the Rev. W. Upton Richards entered into Rest. 6d.

CARTER (Rev. T. T.)
Mercy for the Fallen. Two Sermons in aid of the House of Mercy, Clewer. To which is added an Appeal for the Completion of the House. 1s.
The Divine Service. Preached at the Anniversary of the Consecration of S. John the Evangelist's, Bovey Tracey. 6d.

CARTER (Rev. T. T.)
The Whitsun Consecration Festival at All Saints'. Preached at All Saints', Margaret Street, on the fourth Anniversary of its Consecration. 6d.
The Church's Mission. A Sermon preached at the Parish Church of S. George in the East. 6d.
The Church Union within the Church. Preached on behalf of the English Church Union. 4d.
Fellowship with the Saints. Preached at All Saints', Margaret Street, on All Saints' Day, 1861. 6d.
The True Freedom of Religious Inquiry. A Sermon preached at All Saints', Margaret Street, on the Anniversary Festival of the Guild of the Most Blessed Saviour. Natal. 8vo., 1s.
The Church's Present Work. A Sermon preached at S. Mary Magdalene, Paddington. 8vo., 6d.

CHAMBERLAIN'S (Rev. T.) The Glories of Christ and His Church. A Sermon preached before the University of Oxford. 6d.

CONFRATERNITY OF THE BLESSED SACRAMENT SERMONS :
The Union of the Natural and Supernatural Substances in the Holy Eucharist analogous to that of the Human and Divine Natures in the Incarnation. By the Rev. J. C. Chambers, M.A. 6d.
The Bereaved Comforted. By the Rev. T. T. Carter. M.A. 6d.
Eucharistic Adoration considered as an evidence of Faith and an Impulse of Love. By the Rev. W. U. Richards, M.A. 4d.
The "Reasonable Service." By Alfred Bowers Evans, D.D., Rector of S. Mary-le-Strand. 6d.

COURTENAY (Rev. and Hon. C. L.)
The Presence of Christ with His Ministers, and in Holy Places. 1s.
Unity. A Sermon preached in S. John's, Torquay, on the Opening of the Chancel of the New Church. 6d.

DYKES' (Rev. J. B.) Natural and Spiritual Life. A Sermon preached in Durham Cathedral. 3d.

FLOWERS (Rev. W. B.)
Choral Services and Ritual Observances. Two Sermons, with an Address on the Present Troubles in the Church, preached at Bovey Tracey. 1s.
"The Works of the Lord are Great." A Thanksgiving Sermon. 6d.

FORBES (Rev. G. H.)
"Loose him, and let him go;" or, the Benefit of Absolution. A Sermon. 3d.
"Jesus Wept." A Sermon. 1s.

FOWLER'S (Rev. C. A.) The Church the Bond of Brotherhood. A Club Sermon. 6d.

GUINNESS'S (Rev. E.) Jesus Weary with His Journey. A Sermon preached in S. Michael's Church, Brighton. 3d.

JENNER'S (Bishop) The Grace of Holy Orders and its Correlative Obligations. A Visitation Sermon. 6d.

KEBLE'S (Rev. J.) The Strength of Christ's Little Ones. 6d.

KING (Rev. BRYAN.)
The Recovery of the Lost Sheep of the Church of England by Home Missions in her Large and Destitute Parishes. A Sermon preached at the Opening of the Calvert Street Mission Chapel. 6d.
A Warning against the Sin of Marriage. A Sermon. 6d.

LEE (Rev. F. G.)
The Progress of the Church. A Sermon. 6d.
The Truth as it is in Jesus. Preached at S. Martin's, Leicester, at the Opening of the Lent Assizes, 1861. 6d.

LIDDON'S (Rev. H. P.) The Aim and Principles of Christian Missions. Preached at the Anniversary of S. George's Mission. 4d.

LINDSELL'S (Rev. and Hon. B.) The Inspiration of Holy Scripture as not merely containing but being the Word of God. Preached at S. Paul's, Knightsbridge. 6d.

MACKENZIE'S (Rev. G.) Receiving from God, not giving to God, the Central Idea of Holy Communion. A Few Plain Words addressed to Communicants and Non-communicants. 4d.

MARRIOTT'S (Rev. C.) God and not System the Strength of the Church. Preached at Kemerton on the Dedication Festival. 6d.

MILNER'S (Rev. J.) The Intermediate State; or the State of the Soul between the Death and Resurrection of the Body. Two Sermons. 6d.

MONRO'S (Rev. E.) Home and Colonial Missions. Two Sermons. 1s.

MORRIS'S (Rev. T. E.) God wonderful in His holy places. A Sermon preached at the Re-opening of Eisher Church. 6d.

MURRAY'S (Rev. J.) S. Andrew an Example. A Sermon preached on S. Andrew's Day, 1841. 6d.

NEALE (Rev. J. M.)
"He said, Come." A Sermon preached at the Dedication Festival of S. Matthias', Stoke Newington. 6d.

Neale (Rev. J. M.)
  Sermon. Preached in the Oratory of
  S. Margaret's, East Grinsted. 4th
  edition. 6d.
  Deaconesses, and Early Sisterhoods.
  Two Sermons, preached in the Ora-
  tory of S. Margaret's, East Grin-
  sted. 4d.

Newland's (late Rev. H.) The Two-edged
  Sword of God. A Sermon preached
  on the Day of Humiliation. 3d.

Pearson's (Rev. W. H.) Apostolic Treatment of Divisions in the Church. 1s.

Polehampton's (Rev. J.) Confession in
  the Church of England exceptional; not
  the rule, permitted not commanded.
  Two Sermons. 6d.

Prevost's (Rev. Sir George, Bart.) The
  Restoration of Churches, and the Walk
  in the Spirit. Two Sermons, the second
  by the Rev. C. E. Kennaway. 6d.

Pusey (Rev. E. B.)
  Increased Communions. A Sermon.
  3d.
  "Do all to the Lord Jesus." A Sermon. 3d.

Richardson's (Rev. W.) God's Call of His
  Ministers. A Sermon preached in 1711.
  Reprinted. 4d.

Richardson (Rev. W. M., B.A.) Ritual;
  a Lecture on Churches, their Structure
  and Ornaments; Ministers, their Position and Vestments; the Holy Eucharist and its orderly Celebration. 8vo.,
  1s.

Russell's (Rev. J. F.) Obedience to the
  Church in things Ritual. 6d.

Sermons to Boys.
  The Sin of Consolation. Two Sermons
  to the Boys of All Saints' School,
  Bloxham, 1864. By the Rev. E. J.
  Manning and the Rev. R. Hake. 6d.
  Observance of Fast Days by School-
  boys. A Sermon by the Rev. J. W.
  Hewett, M.A. 6d.
  Vindications the ruin of Body and Soul.
  Two Sermons preached in the Cha-
  pel of S. Peter's, College, Radley.
  By the Rev. R. C. Singleton, M.A.
  4d.

Sisters of Bethany. Three Sermons preached
  at the Chapel Royal, Windsor Great
  Park. 6d.

Skinner (Rev. J.)
  The Priest's Call. A Sermon for Ember
  Days. 1d.
  The Stewards of the Mysteries of God.
  A Sermon for Ember Days. 3d.

Tindal (Rev. J. H.) Unity and Co-opera-
  tion amongst its Members the Strength
  of the Mystical Body of Christ. A
  Sermon preached at East Molly, on
  the occasion of Opening the National
  Schools. 3d.

Toze (Rev. T.)
  "I thirst." A Sermon preached during Lent, in the Parish Church of
  Sleaford. 1s.
  Labour, Learning, and Religion; or,
  the Union of Secular and Religious
  Education. A Sermon preached
  on behalf of the National Schools.
  1s.

Wilberforce (Bishop.)
  Christ the Healer. A Sermon preached
  on the Opening of the New Building of the House of Mercy, Clewer.
  1s.
  "Cast in Mud," or the Poison rendered
  Harmless. A Sermon preached at
  the Laying the Foundation Stone
  of the College Chapel of S. John's,
  Hurstpierpoint. 1s.

Wordsworth (Right Rev. J. A., Bp. of Sly.)
  The Commission and the Promise. A
  Sermon preached at a General Or-
  dination held by the Lord Bishop
  of Oxford. 6d.
  The Throne of David, and the breadth
  of the Divine Commandments.
  Two Sermons on behalf of the Fund
  for building new Schools. 6d.
  The Diversity of Christian Holiness. A
  Sermon preached at Bristol in be-
  half of the Grateful Society. 6d.
  The Building of Gold and of Stubble.
  An Ordination Sermon. 6d.
  The Hidden Manna. A Sermon preached
  at All Saints', Margaret Street, on
  the day after the Consecration. 6d.

Wray's (Rev. C.) The Moral Consequences
  of a False Faith. 6d.

TRACTS, ETC.

LONDON PAROCHIAL TRACTS.

1 Conversion, in Two Parts.   2d., or 14d. per 100.
2 Be One Again. An Earnest Entreaty from a Clergyman to his People to Unite in Public Worship. 1d., or 7s. per 100.
3 The Church a Family; or, a Letter from a Clergyman to the Parishioners upon their Blessings and Duties as Members of the Household of God. 1½d., or 10s. 6d. per 100.
4 Advice to Christian Parents. 1d., or 7s. per 100.
5 The Privilege of Daily Service. 1d., or 7s. per 100.
6 The Church Service and Church Music. 1d., or 7s. per 100.
7 A Few Words to Choristers. ½d., or 3s. 6d. per 100.
8 The Mystery of Godliness. 1d., or 7s. per 100.
9 A Few more Words to Choristers. ½d., or 3s. 6d. per 100.
10 The Worship of the Body; being a Few Plain Words about a Plain Duty. 1d., or 7s. per 100.
11 The Use of Confirmation. 2d., or 14s. per 100.
12 On Almsgiving. ½d., or 3s. 6d. per 100.
13 The Way to become Rich. ½d., or 3s. 6d. per 100.
14 A Popular View of Anglo-Catholicism and Anglo-Catholics. 1d.
15 On the Reverence we ought to show in the House of God. ½d.
16 On Unchastity before Marriage. 1d. or 7s. per 100.
17 Amy, the Factory Girl. ½d., or 3s. 6d. per 100.
18 On Almsdeeds. ½d., or 3s. 6d. per 100.
19 How to Spend the Lord's Day Profitably. ½d., or 2s. 9d. per 100.
20 Conditions of Prayer. ½d., or 3s. 6d. per 100.
21 A Few Words to the Parents of National School Children. 1d.
22 The Misery of Sin. By the Rev. R. G. Boodle. 1d.
23 The Danger of Sin. By the same Author. 1½d.
24 The Object of this Life. By the same Author. 1d.
25 On Fasting. By the Rev. Frederick Pownder. 2d.
26 Thoughts on Turning to the East at the Creed. ½d.
27 Bravery; What is it? 1d.
28 A Watchman's Words in time of danger. 1d.

POPULAR TRACTS, Illustrating the Prayer Book of the Church of England.

1 The Baptismal Services. New Edition. 2d.
2 The Dress of the Clergy, with an Illustration. New Edition. 2d.
3 The Burial Service. With an Appendix on Modern Burials, Monuments, and Epitaphs, containing Seven Designs for Headstones, and an Alphabet for Inscriptions. 6d.
4 The Ordination Services. 4d.

TRACTS ON CHURCH PRINCIPLES. By the Rev. J. R. West.

1 On the Present Grievous loss of Christian Unity. 1d.
2 On the Submission Due to Lawful Authority. 1d.
3 The Apostolic Succession. 1½d.
4 The Apostolic Succession: An Anecdote, showing that all Persons hold the doctrine though they may say they do not. 1½d.
5 What Place of Worship is it my Duty to Attend? 1½d.
6 On the right of calling public assemblies for Divine Worship. 1d.
7 On the nature of a Sacrament. 1½d.
8 The Doctrine of Baptism. 1½d.
9 On the Doctrine of the Holy Eucharist. 1½d.
10 Instructions for Confirmation. 1½d.
11 On the Church. 1d.
12 Reasons for being a Churchman. 1½d.
    Nos. 1 to 12, cloth, 1s. 6d.

MISSION TRACTS. By the Rev. George Body. ½d. each, or 2s. 6d. per 100.

1 Are you at peace with God?
2 Prayer for Mercy.
3 Self-Examination.
4 Confession. Part 1.

5 Confession. Part 2.
6 Jesus our Peace.
7 Salvation by Faith.
8 Praise.

WRAWBY VILLAGE DIALOGUES. By the Rev. J. R. West.

1 Concerning Self-Deception in Religion. 1d.
2 Concerning the words "Believe and be saved." 1d.
3 On the Nature of Conversion. 1d.
4 On the one only Service ordered for us all by the Lord Himself. 1½d.
5 Concerning the Most Holy Communion. 1½d.
6 On the Necessity of the Holy Communion of the Body and Blood of Christ. 1½d.

7 On Ritualism. 1½d.
8 On Church and Chapel, showing the Fundamental Difference between a Churchman and a Dissenter. 1d.
9 On the Essential Principle of Christian Unity. 1d.
10 On Three Chief Articles of Christian Unity. One Baptism, One Altar, One Bishop. 1d.
11 The Same Subject Continued.
12 On Objections and Difficulties.

PARISH TRACTS. In 1 vol., price 2s. 6d. cloth, or in separate parts.

1 Wandering Willie, the Sponsor. 2d.
2 Dermot, the Unbaptized. 3d.
3 Old Robert Gray. 3d.
4 The Ministration of Public Baptism of Infants to be used in the Church. 4d.
7 A Word of Counsel to the Parents of Children attending Parochial Schools. 1d.

8 Little Betsy, A Village Marmtic. 2d.
9 Mabel Bread, A Tale of the Burial Service. 2d.
10 A Plain Sermon respecting Godfathers and Godmothers. 1d.
Nos. 1, 2, 3, 8, and 9, bound together, limp cloth, 1s. 6d.

BOYNE HILL TRACTS.

1 What must I do to be saved? 2d.
2 Conversion. 2d.
3 The Bible and the Prayer Book. 1½d.

4 The Church the Pillar of the Truth. 1½d.
5 Prayer and Preaching. 2d.
6 The Christian Priesthood. 2d.

TRACTS UPON MATTERS OF CHRISTIAN FAITH AND DUTY.
Edited by the Rev. Orby Shipley. 1d. each, or 7s. per 100, 16 pp. 8vo., or 24 pp. 24mo.

1 Of the Calendar of the English Church.
2 Prayers on the Passion.
3 Lives of the Black Letter Saints.
4 Prayers and Hymns before and after Holy Communion.

5 Family Prayers for a Week: from the Prayer Book.
6 Hymns on the Holy Communion.
7 Private Prayers for a Week.
8 The Apostles' Creed.
9 Reasons of the Church—Advent.

FOUR-PAGE TRACTS, suited also for Tract Covers. 3s. 6d. per 100; complete in wrapper, 6d.

1 Scripture Rules for Holy Living.
2 Baptism and Registration.
3 George Herbert.
4 Dreamland.
5 Songs for Labourers.
6 Plain Directions for Prayer, with a few Forms.

7 Reasons for Daily Service.
8 Easter Songs.
9 The Good Shepherd.
10 Morning and Evening Hymns.
11 A Few Reasons for Keeping the Fasts and Festivals.
12 The Church Calendar.

TRACTS FOR PAROCHIAL DISTRIBUTION. By the late Rev. E. J. B. Hughes, Curate of Lythe, and Reaction Holme. 2d. the set, or 14s. per 100.

Holy Baptism.
On the necessity of frequenting the Holy Communion.
What I would do were I a Sponsor.

How to spend the Lord's Day profitably.
What ought I to do in order to receive the full benefits of public worship?
Why I do not go to Meeting.

ON BAPTISM.

The Doctrine of Christian Baptism. By the Rev. J. R. West. 1½d.

Holy Baptism. By the Rev. E. J. R. Hughes. 6d.

A Dialogue upon Baptism. 3d.

The Holiness of a Christian Child; being an Earnest Appeal to all Christian Parents on the Regeneration of their Children in the Sacrament of Baptism. 2d.

The Temples of the Holy Ghost; being a second Earnest Appeal to Parents. 2d.

A Few Plain Words on Baptismal Regeneration. By the Rev. J. Milner. 3d.

Infant Baptism, a Letter to Anabaptists. By the Rev. H. Newland. 1d.

A Manual for Unbaptized Children preparatory to Baptism. 2d.

Sponsor's Remembrance Card. 1d.

A Manual for Unbaptized Adults preparatory to Baptism. 3d.

A Catechism: that is to say, an instruction preparatory to Baptism to be learned by such as are of Riper Years, and able to answer for themselves. 3d.

The Baptismal Service with Explanations. 4d.

What I would do were I a Sponsor. 1s. 9d. per 100.

A Plain Sermon respecting Godfathers and Godmothers. 1d.

Dermot the Unbaptised. 3d.

Wandering Willie, the Sponsor. 2d.

The Sponsor's Duty, for giving to Sponsors at the time of Baptism. 3s. 6d. per 100. On card, rubricated, 1d.

ON CONFIRMATION.

Instructions for Confirmation. By the Rev. J. R. West. 1½d.

An Instruction on Confirmation. 3d.

The Seal of the Lord. A Catechism on Confirmation. By the Bishop of Brechin. 1½d.

Questions and Answers on Confirmation. 1d.

Instructions about Confirmation. 1d.

The Use of Confirmation. By the Rev. W. Gresley. 3d.

A Manual for Christians Unconfirmed. 2d.

Helps for Confirmation and First Communion. 6d.

Plain Instructions on Confirmation. By the Rev. G. R. Fryann. 1d.

Seven Duties following after Confirmation. On card, ½d.

The Laying on of Hands. 4d.

Catechetical Exercise on the Confirmation Service. By the Rev. G. J. Davies. 6d.

Confirmation, its Duties and its Privileges. An Address by the late Bishop of Exeter. 1d.

Meditations on Confirmation. By the Bishop of Calcutta. 3d.

Short Devotions for those who desire to be Confirmed. 1d.

A Manual for Confirmation and First Communion. By the Rev. E. A. Suckling. 6d.

A Guide to Confirmation and Holy Communion. By R. Brett. 6d.

The following have been printed separately from the Rev. H. Newland's Lectures on Confirmation and First Communion:—

Special Lectures on matters of Catechism, addressed to the Catechumens and their Sponsors in the School-room or in the Church on Week-day Evenings; with Questions for Self-examination on the Commandments. 48 pages, 6d.

The Questions may be had separately.

Conversations. 1. The Meaning of Confirmation. 2. The Use of Confirmation. 3. Dangers of Habitual Communion. 4. Lead us not into Temptation. 5. The Lord's Supper. 6. Sacramental Grace. 54 pages, 6d.

Heads of Catechetical Instruction. 1d.

Hymns for Confirmation. 1d.

Letter on Infant Baptism. 1d.

Certificates of Baptism, &c. For pasting into Prayer-Books, &c. 3s. 6d. per 100.

Lecture on the Communion Service, delivered in the week preceding the Celebration: Sermon at the Celebration of the Holy Communion. The Church, a Sermon addressed to those who were lately Catechumens, but who, having been Confirmed, have just been admitted to their First Communion. 24 pages, 6d.

Confirmation as it is in the Church of England. 3d.

ON HOLY COMMUNION.

The Doctrine of the Holy Eucharist. By the Rev. J. R. West. 1½d.

Thoughts about Holy Communion. Reprinted from the "Old Church Porch." 1d.

A Few Plain Words on the Office of Holy Communion. 3d.

The Teaching of the Holy Scripture concerning the Lord's Supper. 2d.

The Scriptural Doctrine of the Holy Communion. By the Rev. W. Nevins. 2d.

The Necessity of Frequenting the Holy Communion. By the Rev. E. J. R. Hughes. 6d.

The Christian Sacrament and Sacrifice, from the Works of the Rev. John Wesley. Edited by the Rev. W. Gresley. 3d.

Some Instructions on the Holy Communion. 1d.

Reasons for Partaking of the Sacrament of the Body and Blood of Christ, and Reasons for not Partaking. 4d.

An Earnest Address on Frequent Communion, especially addressed to the Lately Confirmed. 1d.

A Few Words after First Communion. By W. N. G. ½d.

A Manual for Communicants, being an Assistant to a Devout and Worthy Reception of the Holy Communion. 3d., unabridged 6d.

A Guide to the Eucharist. 4d.

The Eucharistic Month. 8d., cloth 1s.

A Manual, containing Directions and Suitable Devotions for those who remain in Church during the Celebration of the Holy Communion, but do not Communicate. 6d.

Litany for the use of Communicants. 2d.

Form of Self-Examination, with Prayers preparatory to the Holy Communion. 2d.

Hymns on the Holy Communion. By the Rev. Orby Shipley. ½d.

A Few Words on the Blessed Sacrament of the Lord's Supper. Card 2d.

"Art not thou also one of this Man's disciples?" A Tract upon the Holy Communion. 2d.

Prayers and Hymns before and after Holy Communion. By the Rev. Orby Shipley. 1d.

MISCELLANEOUS TRACTS.

Address to the Patients of a Hospital, from the Chaplain. 1d.

Baird's (Rev. W.) Hints for the Formation and Management of Bible Classes. 2d.

Bible, and the Bible only, the Religion of Protestants. By the Rev. J. M. Neale. 4d.

Catholic Reasons for rejecting the Modern Pretensions and Doctrines of the Church of Rome. By the Rev. Cecil Wray. 2d.

Congregational Independents; an Inquiry into their Faith and Practice. By the Rev. H. Wray. 3d.

Church of England the best Church; or, Fifteen Reasons for being a Churchman. By Edwin Caldwell. 20th edition. 2d.

Church's Shadow. By the Rev. E. Tomlins. 1½d.

Do you remember Ascension Day? 1s. 6d. per 100.

Devotional Use of the Church Service. 1s. 6d. per 100.

Due and Lowly Reverence to be done by all at the mention of the Holy Name of Jesus in the time of Divine Service. 1d.

Earnest Exhortation to Confession, addressed to all Sinners who having grievously offended the Divine Majesty, desire by Penitence to destroy the hated Past. 3d.

Explanation of the Commination Service. By the Rev. H. Dunwell. Price 1d.

Faith and Works; or, the Teaching of the Bible the Teaching of the Church. 6d.

Farm Lads, and how to help them. By a Tenant Farmer. 1d.

Few Words about going to Church. ½d.

Few Plain Words about what every Christian ought to know, believe, and do in order to be saved. ½d.

Few Plain Words to Labouring Lads about their Leisure Time. 1d.

Future Communion Service of the Church of England, as rendered from the Primitive Apostolic Liturgies of Catholic Antiquity. 6d.

Few Plain Words to Churchgoers. ½d.

Few Plain Words about the Apostolical Succession. By the Rev. J. Milton. 1d.

Sequel to Ditto. 2d.

Few Words addressed to a Woman after Childbirth. 1d.

Sequel to Ditto. 6d.

Harvest Festival at Lilbrook. 2d.

Important Truths for Important Times: the Bible, the Prayer Book, and the Church. By the Rev. A. J. Piggott. 2d.

Increase of Romanism in England. By the Rev. Henry Newland. 3d.

Jesuitism in the Church. A brief address to Churchmen, pointing out the true quarter in which, if any where, we are now to look for it. 1d.

Layman's Guide to the Occasional Services of the Church. 2d.

Letter of Advice to all the members of the Church of England to come to the Divine Service, Morning and Evening, every Day. ½d.

Lost Sisters Found. Three Tracts for distribution among the Fallen. 3d.

Letter to the Members of the Methodist Society in the Parish of ———. From the Clergyman of the Parish. 2d.

Mann's (W. F.) What is a True Churchman?
1½d.

———— What Day is it? A Few **Plain**
Words on Good Friday. 1d.

Meditations for Passion and Holy Weeks.
By R. B. 1d.

On the Vessels, Colours, Vestments, and
Incense, used at the Celebration of the
Holy Communion, 2nd edition, with
Additions. 1d.

One Mind and One Mouth. **A Tract for**
English Churchmen. 2d.

"One and All," or the Disintegration of
Society; and some of its Remedies.
By the Rev. H. Newland. 2d.

Place where Prayer was wont to be made;
being the Prayer Book's Plea for Daily
Prayer in the Church. By the Rev. R.
Tomkins. 1½d.

Plain Observations upon the Right of Private Judgment. 6d.

Poems for Young and Loving Hearts. By
the Rev. Edmund Worsledge. Price 4d.

Pollock's (Rev. J. S.) What Ritual has God
appointed? 1d.

———— Pastoral Advice of the Rev. John
Wesley, M.A. Twentieth Thousand. 1d.

———— Infant Baptism in the Bible. 1d.

Prayer Book of the Church of England, and
its Forms and Ceremonies. An Address
by the Rev. A. J. Pigott. 6d.

Reasons for being a Churchman. By the
Rev. J. R. West, M.A. 4d.; cheap
edition, 1½d.

Saving Faith viewed in reference to the
teaching of the Rev. R. Aitken and
others. 3d.

Short History of the Mormonites; with an
Account of the Real Origin of the Book
of Mormon. By the Rev. John Frere. 3d.

Social Sin, the. 1d.

Songs and Ballads for Manufacturers. By
the Rev. J. M. Neale. 3d.

Spiritual Wedlock; a full account of the Nature of Christian Marriage. Price 3d.

Unity. A Lecture delivered before Dissenters and others. By the Rev. R. F.
W. Molesworth. 3rd edition. 6d.

What the Bible says to Servants. By
J. R. V. 1½d.

What must I do to be Saved? 1½d.

What Plan of Salvation has the Church of
England taught her Children? By a
Layman. 1d.

CERTIFICATE CARDS OF CONFIRMATION, &c.

A Memorial of Baptism, Confirmation, and
Holy Communion. Printed in colours
with centre cross. 1d.

In Memoriam Cards. Printed in Chromo-
Lithography, with gold or silver borders. 3d., or 2s. per doz.

The Confirmation Medal. 6d.

Certificates of Confirmation and Holy Communion. Printed in red and black, 1d.,
or 7s. per 100.

Certificates of Baptism, Confirmation, and
First Communion. On a large Card.
2d., or 14s. per 100.

Card for admission to Confirmation. 2s. 6d.
per 100.

Certificate of Confirmation and Communion, on a beautifully Ornamented
large Card. 2d.; also new design, 3d.

Certificates of Baptisms and Burials. 3s. 6d.
per 100.

School Check Card. 2s. 6d. per 100.

Notice of Baptism. 4s. 6d. per 100.

My Duty at the time of Confinement. 2s. 6d.
per 100.

Plain Reasons for worshipping God in His
Temple. 1d.

How to Spend Sunday Well and Happily.
1d., or 7s. per 100.

Address to Parents of Children at National
and Sunday Schools. 1d.

SHEETS.

Ten Reasons why I love my Church, and
Ten Reasons why I love my Prayer
Book. 1½d.

Ten Plain Reasons why I **love my Bible.**
1½d.

Directions for the time of Dressing. 1d.

Devotions for the time of Undressing. 1d.

The Daily Life of the Christian Child. 1d.

The Last Sleep of the Christian Child. 1d.

Harmony of the Holy Week. 1d.

A Challenge to Dissenters of whatever de-
nomination. 2s. per 100.

Directions for the Lord's Day. 2s. per 100.

Infant Baptism a Moral Certainty. 1s. 2d.
per 100.

A Score of Doubts. 1s. 3d. per 100.

The Bishop of New Jersey on the Offertory.
2s. 6d. per 100.

LEAFLETS, &c.

By the Rev. J. S. B. Monsell, LL.D.

"Blest Sign of Man's Redemption." Verses on the Cross. 4d. per dozen.
Ditto on large card with Photograph of "Faith." 6d.
No Sect on Earth; a Sequel to "No Sect in Heaven." 6d. per doz.

Verses on Lent. 4d. per doz.
Eucharistic Verses. 1d.
"His Light my Guide." On Card. 1d.
Ditto set to Music by Dr. Gauntlett. On Card. 3d.

Prayers before and after Service. 4d. per doz.
On Behaviour at Church. 4d. per doz.

Verses on the Prayer Book, with space for date of Baptism, Confirmation, and Holy Communion. 4d. per doz.

CLASSIFIED PRICE LIST OF REWARD BOOKS,

AND

BOOKS FOR LENDING LIBRARIES.

PENNY.

THE SEVEN CORPORAL WORKS OF MERCY.—In Seven Tales. In a Packet, or bossd in ornamental cover, 6d.

THE SEVEN SPIRITUAL WORKS OF MERCY.—In a Packet, or bound in ornamental cover, 6d.

THE HALF-HOLIDAY. A Packet of Six Tales, containing Six Different Ways of Spending a Half-Holiday. In a Packet, 6d.

THE YOUNG SOLDIERS, or THE DOUBLE BIRTHDAY; and other Tales. A packet of Seven Tales, or bound, 6d.

THE SCHOLAR'S NOSEGAY. Being a series of Tales and Conversations on Flowers. In a neat box, containing 10, 1s.; or cloth gilt edges, 1s. 6d.

FLOWERS AND FRUIT, ETC. For Little Children. In a neat box, 1s.; or cloth gilt edges, 1s. 6d.

STORIES AND LESSONS ON THE FESTIVALS, FASTS, AND SAINTS' DAYS. In 89 little books, 2s. 6d. the set. In 3 vols., cloth, 2s.

Vol. I.	Vol. II.	Vol. III.
Advent	2. Andrew	5. Mark
Christmas Day	6. Thomas	22. Philip and James
Epiphany	3. Stephen	8. Barnabas
Ash Wednesday	5. John the Evangelist	3. John the Baptist
Good Friday	The Holy Innocents	5. Peter
Easter Eve	Circumcision	1. James
Easter Day	Conversion of S. Paul	3. Bartholomew
Ascension Day	Purification	6. Matthew
Whitsunday	8. Matthias	2. Michael & All Angels
Trinity Sunday	Annunciation	8. Luke
		28. Simon and Jude
		All Saints

TALES OF MY DUTY TOWARDS MY NEIGHBOUR. 32mo., cloth, 1s.

THE LITTLE COMFORTERS, and other Tales. In a packet, or cloth, 1s.

The Two Ways of Ruth Martin	Little Ellen, or the Sick Child; and Death	How must I behave? or, My Duty to my Neighbour
Rachel Ford; or the Little Girl who tried to be Good	Sunday	Jennie's Christmas
The Little Comforters	The Little Street Sweeper	John Dobson; or, What a Boy may do
The Four Seasons	The Rose Tree; or, Dinah's divoce	The Little Faithful Servant
The Coward		

HOLIDAY HOURS. A Packet of Thirteen Reward Books, with Vignettes, by the author of "The Little Comforters." 1s. in cloth, gilt; or separately in a packet.

Little Timothy Martin; or, the First Lie.	The Circumcision of our Year's Day.	The Emigrants.
The Way of Peace; or, the History of Old Nanny.	Love and Innocence.	The Midnight Flight. A Story of Ancient Times.
The Bricklayer's Accident; or, the Good Doctor.	The Little Nurse-girl; or Thoughtful Care.	The Only Child; or, Beatrice and Mary.
The Happy Sisters.	The Orphan Apprentice; or, Temptation Resisted.	The Confirmation of Jessie and Ralph.
Little Willie Grant.		

CHAPTERS ON PLANTS; or, Marion's Herbal. A Packet of Thirteen Books. Reprinted from the *Churchman's Companion.* 1s. in cloth gilt; or separately, in a packet.

CHAPTERS ON ANIMALS; or, Annie Grant's Playmates. A Packet of Thirteen Reward Books. Reprinted from the *Churchman's Companion.* 1s. cloth gilt.

THE TWO BIRTHDAYS. AND OTHER TALES. A Packet of Six small Reward Books, by the author of "Harold, a Ghost Story with a Moral." 6d. in packet or cloth.

The Two Birthdays.	Carelessness sometimes Dishonesty.
Mary's Sorrow.	Henry and the Sheep.
"I wish."	The Little Fairies.

One Penny.

In packets of 6, price 6d.
Allotment Ground
Clerly and Agnes
First Failing
Root of Bitterness
Sunday in the Country
What is Liberty?

How to be a Martyr
Hymns for Infant Children
Questions on Christian Doctrines and Practice

Twopence.

In Packets of 13. Price 2s.
Brother's Sacrifice
Cat and her Kittens
Dishonesty
Dumb Boy
Few Prayers and a Few Words about Prayer
How to be Useful and Happy
"I am so happy"
Little Lace Girl
Little Stories for Little Children
Margaret Hunt
Ravens
Sprained Ancle
Two Sheep

Annandale
Boy Martyr
Child's Mission, The
Lucy Ford
Mary Wilson, or Self-Denial
Minnie Harlow
Pattie Grahame
Rose Eglinton
Stray Donkey, The
Story of a Primrose
Story of a Promise that was kept
Tale of a Tortoise
Thrift

Threepence.

Blind Curate's Child.
Cooper's Few Hints to Mothers
Daily Life of the Christian Child
Daisy
Easy Catechism on the Old Test.
Explanation of Scripture Terms
Glimpse of the Unseen
Hymns for Little Children
Lost Sheep of the Christian Child
Lessons for every Day in the Week
Life of Dr. Allestree
Moral Songs
Neale's Hymns for Children.
    1st Series
Ditto   2nd Series
Ditto   3rd Series
Narrative Hymns
Simpson, the Fisherman
Stout John
Two Suspicion
Willy Morgan

Fourpence.

1st Series.—In a Packet of 13. 4s.
Annie's Grave
Beating the Bounds
Bonfire
Cottage in the Lane
Drunkard's Boy, The
Hallowmas Eve
Mary Cooper
Pancake Bell
Railroad Boy
Robert Lee
Ringers, The
Sunday Walk and a Sunday Talk
Wake, The
2nd Series.—In a packet of 13. 4s.
Christian Heroism

Consolation, or Benefits of Intercessory Prayer
Day's Pleasure
Dream of S. Perpetua
Ellen Meyrick
Flora and her Children
Legend of S. Dorothea
Little Miners
Little Willie, the Lame Boy
Miss Peck's Adventures
Secret, The
Siege of Nisibis
Try Again

Annie's Cross
Alice Parker
Annie Merton
Autumn and Spring
Bereavement
Boy Prince of Mercia
Choristers of S. Mary's
Christian's Converse
Churchyard Gardening
Cornelia; or, Self-Will
Corner Stone
Easy Lessons on Church Service
Forsaken
Gabriel's Dream and Waking
George Malinge
Harold, a Ghost Story
Holystone, or the Two Penitents
Horsceck's Primitive Christians
Hugh
Island Choir
John Borton
Kitty Scramming
Land of Flies
Laura F.
Legend of S. Christopher
Lily of the Valley
Little Mary; or, the Captain's Gold Ring
Little Ruth Gray
Little Walter, the Lame Chorister
Lost One Found
Memoir of Helen Inglis
Miss Chanter's Work

Fourpence. (Cond.)

My Dream
My Godmother's Letter
Neale's Two Hens
Old Oliver Dale
Our Little Kathleen
Pay next Week
Perseverance
Pitney's Cottage Economy
Pride of Rose Lynn
Rags and Tatters
Ruth Digby
K. John the Evangelist's Day
Sibyl Marchant
Smith's Church Catechism Illustrated
Strength and Weakness
Sunday of the People in France
Tale of a Cotton Gown
The Error Corrected
Upward and Onward
Walter the Convict
Willie Grant
Worshipping the Lord in the Beauty of Holiness
Young Anglers of Vichy

Sixpence.

Amy, the King's Daughter
Betty Corewell and her Grandchildren
Bishop's Visit
Book for Fairies
Charley's Trip to the Black Mountain
Charlotte Drew's Pinch
Child's Baptismal Name
Chorister's Fall
Devotions for Schoolboys
Easy Tales for Little Children
Ellen Ashton
Everlasting Hills
Fair and the Confirmation
Father's Hope
Force of Habit
Garden in the Wilderness
George Foster the Page
George Turner
Gerhard's Meditations
Grandfather's Christmas Tale
Hymns for Little Children
Hymns on the Catechism
Is it the best?
Johns' Easy Dictation Lessons
Joy in Duty
Legend of Golden Water
Legend of the Land of Pike
Little Nelly
Little Annie, or Michaelmas Day
Little Stories for Little Children
Lives of Englishmen, 1st Series
Ditto 2nd Series

Manual for Confirmation
Mary Mansfield
Memorial of M. E. D.
Memoir of Elizabeth A——
Mercy Dowmer
Michael the Chorister
Midsummer Eve
Millie's Journal
Mirrors, The
Monro's Nanny
Monro's Story of an Old Coat
Mother's Easter Offering
Mystery of Marking
Neale's Hymns for the Sick
Neglected Opportunity
Nelly Upton
Never too Late to Mend
Nine Shillings a Week
Old Betty, Part I.
Old Betty, Part II.
Old Woman's Story
Old William, or the Longest Day
Path of Life
Peter Noble, the Royalist
Philip Bérant
Plain Reading Lessons from Scripture History
Poems on Old Testament Subjects, Parts I. and II.
Portions of the Psalms
Post-office Window
Precious Stones of the King's House
Progress of the Church since the Reformation
Rachel Ashburn
Ready and Desirous, or a Lent's Lessons
Recollections of a Soldier's Widow
Ruth Osborne
Seven Corporal Works of Mercy
Seven Spiritual Works of Mercy
Shepherds of Bethlehem
Sister's Care. By the Author of "Michael the Chorister."
Sister Rosalie
Stone's Angels
Stories on the Lord's Prayer
Sunset Reverie
Susan Spelman
Subsetting; or, Old Age in Its Glory
Susanna
Ten Commandments in Verse
The Two Friends
Threefold Promise and Threefold Blessing
Trehuraye School
The Twins; or Thy Will be done
Verses for Church Schools
Vicar's Guest
Young Churchman's Alphabet
Young Soldiers, &c.

Eightpence.

Edna Grant
Johns' Easy Dictation Lessons, &c.
Kettlewell's Companion for the Penitent
Low's Translation of the Holy Scriptures
Manuals for Industrial Schools, Cooking
Ditto, Gardening
Ditto, Household Work
Ditto, Needlework
Ditto, Domestic Fowls
Milman's Voices of Harvest
Moral Songs, paper cover
Nelson's Guide to the Holy Communion
Nurse Amy
Taylor's Death, Judgment, Heaven, and Hell
Wilkins' Lecture on Early Church History

Ninepence.

Cousin Rachel, Four Parts
Ken's Practice of Divine Love
Life of Bishop Ball
Life of Jones of Nayland
Milly Wheeler
Progress of the Church since the Reformation, cloth
Sanderson's Christian Contentment
Tower Builders

One Shilling.

Adams' Cressingham
Amy, The King's Daughter, cloth
An Author's Children
Archie's Ambition
Baptismal Vows
Book of Church History
Catechism on the Incarnation.
Chapters on Animals
Chapters on Plants
Charcoal Burners
Child's New Lesson Book
Christmas Dream
Christine's Plain Guide
Christine Servant's Book
Christmas Eve, and other Poems
Christmas Present for Children
Commentary on the Seven Penitential Psalms
Cosin's Private Devotions
Devout Chorister
Drop in the Ocean
Doctrine of the Cross illustrated
Fanny's Flowers

One Shilling. (Cont.)

Flower's Classical Tales
Flower's Tales of Faith and Providence
Flowers and Fruit
Fox's Noble Army of Martyrs
Frederick Gordon
Gentle Influence
Greeley's Treatise on the Church
Harry's Help
Hatherleigh Cross
Heywate's Manual
Higher Claims
Hill's Stories on the Commandments, First Table, cloth
Hopwood's Child's Geography
Hymns for Little Children, cl.
Hymns on the Catechism
In the Choir and out of the Choir
Johns' Questions on the Pentateuch
Ken's Preparatives for Death
Life of Bishop Andrewes
Life of Bishop Wilson
Life of Dr. Hammond
Mercy Downer
Meeting in the Wilderness
Midsummer Eve, cloth
Midsummer Holidays
Milman's Voices of Harvest, cloth
Milman's Way through the Desert
Monro's Dark River, limp cloth
Monro's Combatants, ditto
Monro's Revellers, &c., ditto
Monro's Vast Army, ditto
Monro's Journey Home, do.
Monro's Dark Mountains, do.
Monro's Footprints in the Snow
Monro's Leila
Monro's Harry and Archie
Moral Songs, cloth
Neale's Hymns for Children, cloth
Neale's Hymns for the Sick, cloth
Neale's Christian Heroism
Neale's Christian Endurance
Noble Aim
Nuna's Chart
Old Court House
Paget's E. Antholin's
Patrick's Parable of the Pilgrim
Pearson's Home Tales
Philpot' Catechism on Scriptures
Poems on Old Testament Subjects, Part I. & II. rt.
Prisoners of Craigmaigara
Robert and Ellen
Scholar's Nosegay
Sister Rosalie, cloth

Steps to the Altar
Stories on the Beatitudes
Story of a Dream
Stretton's Catechisms, cloth
Tales of my Duty to my Neighbour
Tales of the Empire
Voyage to the Fortunate Isles
Was It a Dream? and The New Churchyard

One and Sixpence.

Art of Contentment
Beatrice
Charcoal Burners, cloth
Child's New Lesson Book, cloth
Fanny's Flowers, cloth
Galaghems
Grace Alford
Greeley's Holiday Tales, stiff cover
Higher Claims
Ivo and Verena, limp cloth
Monro's Combatants, cl. bds.
Monro's Dark River, do.
Monro's Revellers, &c., do.
Monro's Dark Mountains, do.
Monro's Vast Army, do.
Monro's Journey Home, do.
Monro's Pascal the Pilgrim
Nellie's Care
Parish Tracts, (1 Vols) cloth
Pool's Churches
Pye's Ecclesiastical History
Readings from Holy Scripture
Rockaero's Stories on the Commandments, Second Table
Russell's Lays of the Early Church
Ruth Levinn
Selections from S. Francis de Sales
Stone's Ellen Merton
Tales of the Empire
Taylor's Life of Christ
Vidal's Esther Merle
Was It a Dream? and the New Churchyard, cloth
What we are to Believe
Wilberahem's Kings of Judah

One and Eightpence.

Fasts and Festivals
Greeley's Siege of Lichfield, stiff cover
Greeley's Charles Lever, do.
Moseman's Glossary of Scripture Words.

Two Shillings.

Adams' Silvio
Arden's Manual of Catechetical Instruction

Arnold's History of Ireland
Reed's Lays of the Hebrews
Chapters on Te Deum
Charity at Home
Children of Rose Lynn
Churchman's Companion, Vols. I. to XL. 1st Series
Church Floral Decoration
Flower's Classical Tales
Flower's Tales of Faith and Providence
Fox's Noble Army of Martyrs
Fox's History of Rome
Greeley's Forest of Arden, stiff cover
Greeley's Holiday Tales, cloth
Heywate's Godfrey Davenant
History of Portugal
History of Scotland
Hopwood's Geography
Ivo and Verena
Johns' History of Spain
Johns' Collects and Catechising
Kemple's Soliloquy of the Soul
Ken's Practice of Divine Love
King of a Day
Little Alice
Manger of the Holy Night
Mary and Mildred
Memoirs of an Arm Chair
Minnie's Birthday
Monro's Stories of Cottagers
Neale's Egyptian Wanderers
Neale's Lent Legends
Neale's Christian Endurance
Neale's Christian Heroism
Neale's Deeds of Faith
Neale's Evenings at Sackville College
Neale's Stories from Heathen Mythology
Neale's English History for Children
Neale's Greece
Neale's Mediaeval Hymns
Paget's Luke Sharp
Paget's Hope of the Katzekopfs
Paget's Tales of Village Children, Vol. I.
Ditto, Vol. II.
Poynings; a Tale of the Revolution
Sacred History. Old Test.
Sacred History. New Test.
Scenes in the Lives of Christian Children
Somerford Priory
Steps to the Altar, 32mo.
Tales of Crowbridge Work house
Thinking for Oneself
Trust
Verses for the Christian Year
Vidal's Home Trials
Watson's Catechism on Common Prayer
Winter in the East

Two and Sixpence.

Adams' Fall of Croesus
Adventures of Old Tryggvesson
Baines' English History
Baron's Little Daughter and other Tales
Beginnings of Evil
Child's New Lesson Book, col.
Christian Gentleman's Daily Walk
Companion to Sunday Services
Curate of Cumberworth
Divine Master
Echoes of Old Cornwall
Echoes of our Childhood
Evans' Tales of the British Church
Goodrich's Claudia
Gresley's English Churchman
Holidays at S. Mary's
Lives of Englishmen
Local Legends
Loraine's Lays of Israel
Lord of the Forest and his Vassals
Loving Service
Life, &c., Easy incumbents
Mirror of Young Christians
Neale's Unseen World
Swift of Owlstone Edge
Paget's Christians's Day
Parish Tracts, cloth
Pietas Metrica
Poole's Churches, their structure, &c., cloth
Rainy Mornings with Aunt Mabel
Snowball and other Tales
Snowbound to Cleeberrie Grange
Rosalie and Yvrafe
Reece's Handbook to the Christian Year
Stamps

Three Shillings.

Sylvester Enderby
Tales of a London Parish
Tiny Pollie's Ups and Downs
Village Story for Village Maidens
Walter the Schoolmaster
Williams' Altar, or Meditations in Verse
Whytehead's College Life

Chorister Brothers
Gertrude Dacre
Gresley's Frank's Trip to the Continent
Gresley's Siege of Lichfield
Gresley's Forest of Arden
Gresley's Bernard Leslie, Part I.
Ditto Part II.
Gresley's Coniston Hall
Gresley's Sophron and Neologus
Hicks' Lectures on the Incarnation
Neale's Stories of the Crusades

Three and Sixpence.

Apple Blossom
Alice Beresford
Basil the Schoolboy
Scan's Solitary, or, a Lay from the West
Birthday
Church Floral Decoration, (coloured)
Heygate's William Blake
Ivon
Life of Archbishop Laud
Life of Bishop Hacket
Lucy and Christian Wainwright
Lyra Sanctorum
Maiden Aunt

Memoir of Rev. R. A. Suckling
Monro's Allegories, 1st Series
Monro's Allegories, 2nd Series
Neale's Duchenier, or, the Revolt of La Vendée
One Story by Two Authors
Pollard's Avice
Spiritual Voices from the Middle Ages
Scripture History for the Young
Wilford's Master of Churchill Abbots

Four Shillings.

Hilary S. Magna
Summerleigh Manor
The Churchman's Companion, Vols. I. to VI. Second Series
Ditto, Third Series, Vols. I. to VIII.

Four and Sixpence.

Ion Lester
Life's Search
Scenes of Suburban Life
Selections New and Old

Five Shillings.

Chronicle of Day by Day
Henrietta's Wish
Paget's Warden of Berkingholt
Rockstro's Abbey Lands
Ross's Summer Wanderings
Teale's Lives of English Divines
Wilford's Play and Earnest
Wynnes, The

LONDON : JOSEPH MASTERS AND CO., 78, NEW BOND STREET.